TO PIMP A

Forthcoming in the series:

and many more . . .

To Pimp a Butterfly

Sequoia Maner

BLOOMSBURY ACADEMIC
NEW YORK • LONDON • OXFORD • NEW DELHI • SYDNEY

BLOOMSBURY ACADEMIC
Bloomsbury Publishing Inc
1385 Broadway, New York, NY 10018, USA
50 Bedford Square, London, WC1B 3DP, UK
29 Earlsfort Terrace, Dublin 2, Ireland

BLOOMSBURY, BLOOMSBURY ACADEMIC and the Diana logo are
trademarks of Bloomsbury Publishing Plc

First published in the United States of America 2022
Reprinted in 2022, 2023 (twice)

Library of Congress Cataloging-in-Publication Data

Names: Maner, Sequoia, author.
Title: To pimp a butterfly / Sequoia Maner.
Description: New York : Bloomsbury Academic, 2022. | Series: 33 1/3 | Includes bibliographical references. |
Summary: "This book dives into the sounds, images, and lyrics of To Pimp a Butterfly to suggest that Kendrick
appeals to the psyche of a nation in crisis and embraces the development of a radical political conscience.
Kendrick breathes life into the black musical protest tradition and cultivates a platform for loving resistance.
Combining funk, jazz, and spoken word, the expansive sonic and lyrical geography brings a level of innovation
to a field dominated by the predictability of trap music. More importantly, Kendrick's introspective and
philosophical songs compel us to believe in a future where we gon' be alright!" – Provided by publisher.
Identifiers: LCCN 2021052882 (print) | LCCN 2021052883 (ebook) | ISBN 9781501377471 (paperback) |
ISBN 9781501377488 (epub) | ISBN 9781501377495 (pdf) | ISBN 9781501377501
Subjects: LCSH: Lamar, Kendrick, 1987-. To pimp a butterfly. | Lamar, Kendrick, 1987—Criticism and
interpretation. | Rap (Music)–2011-2020–History and criticism.
Classification: LCC ML420.L2276 M36 2022 (print) | LCC ML420.L2276 (ebook) | DDC 782.421649092–dc23
LC record available at https://lccn.loc.gov/2021052882
LC ebook record available at https://lccn.loc.gov/2021052883

ISBN: PB: 978-1-5013-7747-1
ePDF: 978-1-5013-7749-5
eBook: 978-1-5013-7748-8

Series: 33 ⅓

Typeset by Deanta Global Publishing Services, Chennai, India
Printed and bound in Great Britain

To find out more about our authors and books visit www.bloomsbury.com and sign up for newsletters.

Rap is a technologically sophisticated project in African-American recuperation and revision.
—*Tricia Rose*[1]

Contents

Figures

Preface

This project springs from a personal place and I have been writing toward this book for many years. Kendrick and I are the same age and we grew up a few miles from each other, separated by the blocks that divide Compton and Long Beach (northside). We survived black adolescence in Los Angeles at a time when the state and its agents were determined to instill law and order and consolidate methods of punishment at the cost of many lives. We share the memories of Latasha Harlins, Rodney King, and too many others whose lives were foreshortened by debilitating poverty, brutalizing police forces, and unjust laws. We also share the embodied knowledge that music is capable of soothing a city burned barren by uprising. From what I know, Kendrick and I had vastly different upbringings—his gang-affiliated and dangerous, mine upwardly mobile and shielded—yet we are both shaped by the dramatic climate of black Los Angeles in the age of mass incarceration. We grew into poets who, in our own ways, are both invested in literacy and uplift for black communities.

Kendrick Lamar offers listeners a personal narrative that examines what it means to stay healthy and whole in a system of racial capitalism that negates self-determination and cuts short promising lives. In the popular sphere, Kendrick's music echoes bright against a redundant background of rap clichés by celebrating aliveness and liberating love.[1] The act of introspection and rigorous love are socially and politically transformative, especially for those who have been cast as incapable of reason and as unworthy of receiving care and compassion. I recognize Kendrick as an organic intellectual who is an unparalleled writer and thoughtful performer who crafts philosophical albums with staying power—albums that invite replay and re-listening. As Kendrick says, "I want you to live with it . . . grow with it. At the end of the day, I make albums that have that kind of longevity."[2]

My voice and this book differ from studies in circulation. Marcus J. Moore's book *The Butterfly Effect* provides a stunning chronicle of the artist's rise from adolescence to stardom—Moore's behind-the-scenes account of studio sessions is especially compelling. Other outlets like Cole Cuchna's *Dissect* podcast and the crowdsourced annotation website Genius unpack the layered, complex story that Kendrick composes on *To Pimp a Butterfly*. They each offer great track-by-track and line-by-line breakdowns of the album's narrative. However, in my estimation, too many publications have been invested in translating Kendrick's "enigmatic" mode storytelling in ways that feel like the translation of "blackness" for white readerships, an endeavor in which I have no investment. Instead, I strive to contextualize the artist. I want to celebrate the brilliant hues and textures of Kendrick's dynamic artistry and, for me, so much of this dynamism comes from the citational richness of the music. Legacies, lineages, linkages—this book is obsessed with history because Kendrick Lamar is obsessed with history and because to truly wrestle with his gift is to study that which has shaped his sensibility, a shaping that is conscious and unconscious, contemporary and of the past.

Track Listing

1. Wesley's Theory
2. For Free? (Interlude)
3. King Kunta
4. Institutionalized
5. These Walls
6. u
7. Alright
8. For Sale? (Interlude)
9. Momma
10. Hood Politics
11. How Much a Dollar Cost?
12. Complexion (A Zulu Love)
13. The Blacker the Berry
14. You Ain't Gotta Lie (Momma Said)
15. i
16. Mortal Man

1

Rage

All you are ever told in this country about being black is that it is a terrible, terrible thing to be. Now, in order to survive this, you have to really dig down into yourself and re-create yourself, really, according to no image which yet exists in America.
—*James Baldwin*[1]

To Pimp a Butterfly testifies to pressures facing black men in the recording industry including the allure of materialism and performance of hardness in rap culture. In this chapter, I emphasize how performance poetry magnifies the fractured and deteriorating psyche of a struggling artist and how rage serves as a catalyzing source of creativity. I recover Funkadelic's 1972 album *America's Eats Its Young* as a defining prototype for the rapper to explore truth-telling about selfhood and artistry. I frame Kendrick's industry insights into exploitation, what he calls "pimping," within a long history of black innovation that has been exploited and appropriated, misused and abused.

****

Kendrick Lamar's ascent in popular culture has been swift and high-pitched. Having gained national buzz with his 2012 sophomore project *good kid, m.A.A.d city*, the rapper became a household name and decorated artist with his third album *To Pimp a Butterfly* (2015) and with his fourth release in 2017, *DAMN*, garnered the Pulitzer Prize. Widely regarded to be his magnum opus, *To Pimp a Butterfly* is the album that launched Kendrick into another stratosphere, ranking #1 on lists by nearly every major music outlet including *Pitchfork, Rolling Stone, Complex,* and *Spin*. "To receive 11 [Grammy] nominations and be nominated for Album of the Year, now it feels like the world is listening to us," the rapper excitedly marveled.[2] (Note Kendrick's use of the communal "us," something I'll return to throughout this book.)

For a bona fide rap star, Kendrick navigates celebrity in untraditional ways, primarily through acts of refusal. He keeps no social media accounts and stays out of the gossip circuits. He gives few interviews and keeps a low profile. His infrequent broadcast performances are special viewing events, as are his tours. Kendrick remains an elusive artist who lets the music speak for itself. So, when he became a household name, increased visibility and new demands vexed the artist. The rapper channeled his frustration into song. *To Pimp a Butterfly* is the autobiographical portrait of pivotal life experiences where Kendrick is the protagonist of a story about negotiating two disparate spheres: the Compton homespace that reared him and music industry through which he has elevated. He testifies to the growing pains of a blossoming artist, and listeners gain insight into sources of stress in the rapper's life as he strives for balance between familial obligation and mainstream achievement.

In interviews he has spoken candidly about the sorrow-laden conditions that inspired his masterpiece. Between 2013 and 2014, as he was experiencing unprecedented fame—travelling the world, touring with Kanye, being called one of *the greatest alive*—Kendrick lost three loved ones to the hazards of Compton. While touring on the breakneck success of *good kid, m.A.A.d city*, the rapper received devastating news: his nephew (the son of his best friend) had been shot and killed back home in LA, a loss made unbearable by the promise Kendrick had sworn—to watch over him while his father served out his sentence.

> A friend never leave Compton for profit or leave his best friend
> Little brother, you promised you'd watch him before they shot him
> Where was your antennas?

In this excerpt from the track "u," the rapper battles and berates himself. In his own eyes, he was too caught up in an emergent rap career and, thus, failed to protect his family. As Kendrick hurls curses at himself, listeners bear uncomfortable witness to his struggle with survivor's guilt, the debilitating feelings of shame and regret that come with responsibility to the beloved and bereaved, especially for the high-achieving black individual.

The album feels like a stream of consciousness that has been sifted through, reckoned with, and patterned into art. Cerebral and theatrical, confessional and aspirational, analog and orchestral, *To Pimp a Butterfly* strives for equilibrium in all regards. Balanced against the deep sense of grief spurred by loss is redemptive faith. Like the poem that slowly builds over the course of the record, a narrative about awakening—about exploring one's interior and coming-to-consciousness of one's uniquely divine purpose—comes to light. Dense, spiraling, and even strange, *To Pimp a Butterfly* is difficult in form. Performance poetry. G-funk. Hard bop. Conjuration. The album blends black sound and experimental style for a revelatory listening experience, a unique offering of intellectual and spiritual labor.

The title of Lamar's signature album reflects the artist's primary objective: *To Pimp a Butterfly* examines the intense commodification that informs black expression in the United States and within a global market, and connects this phenomenon to long patterns of exploitation. Kendrick explores the possibilities for men to transform into beautiful butterflies while locked within exploitative institutions and structures, pimped within the music industry and pimped within the US superstructure. Where *Butterfly* is difficult in form, the record is equally difficult in subject for Kendrick exposes the logics of antiblackness in our late capitalist stage by meditating upon the fetishization of black bodies, black sound, and black creativity in the United States. And yet, despite these difficulties, or precisely because of these difficulties, *To*

Pimp a Butterfly is a masterpiece. Released during a time of sociocultural awakening that stirred up strong feelings of shame and longing in an embattled public, Kendrick and his bandmates poignantly capture the fraught yearnings of a transforming nation.

Butterfly is structured as a conceptual album that coheres a story that unfolds track by episodic track. Kendrick proves himself a master writer as the record has all the features of great narrative including an exposition, rising and falling action, a climax and denouement, and a cast of characters with several antagonists to be vanquished. His storytelling is precise and cinematic. The record encourages a start-to-finish listening mode, indicated by the titular poem that slowly reveals itself couplet by couplet on successive songs, finally unfurling to maximum length on the closing track, "Mortal Man." Of this poem that slowly reveals itself, Kendrick reflects, "I wanted a thread that conceptually ties in the songs. I've always been a fan of movie flicks and writers, I just love writers."[3] Kendrick is a lyricist-lover's dream, and his focus on interesting, untraditional narrative composition requires recursive listening—he crafts albums that demand labor on the part of the listener and, in doing so, encourages us to discover and rediscover. In short, the replay value of Kendrick's artistry is *insane.*

The composition process for *Butterfly* unfolded over the course of two years, and the rapper's growth and continued clarity gained during that time is undeniable. Kendrick shows more than lyrical virtuosity in his increased control over the sonic arc of a track—he builds layers of sound on top of each other in stimulating ways, letting the music breathe and percolate in between barrages of meticulously placed words and evocative instrumentation. He says, "My process, it starts from just a bunch of premeditated thoughts . . . and by the time I get into the studio, I have to find the exact sound that triggered the emotion or the idea that I thought about two months ago."[4] In this case, travel to South Africa is the catalyst for building sound from thought. His trip "home" was a life-changing experience that spurred a sonic and philosophical opening that marks *To Pimp a Butterfly* as exquisitely singular. Mark "Soundwav" Spears, TDE (Top Dawg Entertainment) house producer and one of the primary architects of *Butterfly*'s soundscape, remembers that "he took a trip to Africa and something in his mind just clicked. For me, that's when this album really started."[5] Upon returning to the United States to make music, the rapper scratched everything he had been working on (rumored to be two to three albums worth of material) and started fresh from an inspired place. He gathered a group of avant-garde, LA-based jazz musicians around him and hunkered down for a full year to *find the exact sound that triggered the emotion*. The result was *To Pimp a Butterfly*.

I am interested in Kendrick's self-reflective capacities— so much of this record rotates around the notion of agency grasped outside of routinized contexts. In the realm of *Butterfly*, self-determination resists the commodifying forces of capitalism. Salvation won't be found in the market and success is not indexed by an accumulation of wealth. Kendrick is interested in self-love, mental health, healing from trauma, and the discovery of divine alignment. On the role of the artist, Kendrick echoes James Baldwin when he says,

> So, you ask yourself in the midnight hour, "Who am I? Is this really what I'm supposed to be doing? How did I get here? Why am I doing this? What's my responsibility?" It's a real trippy thing, you feel me? And I think it's something that nobody can understand; only an artist can.[6]

Every Nigger Is a Star

As the album's opening track, "Wesley's Theory" does extraordinary work to lay a foundation that Kendrick will elaborate upon and embellish. The first sound that listeners hear is the distinctive crackle of a stylus setting onto a vinyl record, and, collectively, we are attuned to the few glorious moments of anticipatory silence before the music begins. The static of the record player at once signals a nostalgic, soulful dream space and insists upon a linear listening mode, one that unfolds from beginning to end because Kendrick has a story to tell. Sampled crooning from Jamaican singer Boris Gardiner echoes a mantra of black pride that rises in volume—*every nigger is a star*.[7] The sample injects an ambiance of personhood and belonging. For the rapper and for the listener—everyone gathered is somebody. The sample also centers on the subject of stardom for the black artist, a central concern of the album's narrative. Kendrick's first verse occupies the voice of a speaker who dreams of material success in the rap game, a young rapper who avows that "When I get signed, homie I'mma act a fool." Swearing by "platinum on everything," the speaker is giddy with the taste of purchasing power and catalogs his wish list of items including "a brand new Caddy," a "bad bitch," and "a strap" (a gun). It seems that Kendrick has strayed from his lofty ideals and reverted back to the adolescent mentality articulated by his K. Dot persona on *good kid, m.A.A.d city*. With fame has come the desire for typical rap industry status symbols and the occlusion of Kendrick's strong ethical core.

Uncle Sam makes his first appearance on the album as one antagonist in Kendrick's narrative, and not since Ice Cube's *Death Certificate* (1991) have we seen the icon so effectively deployed in rap music. Uncle Sam entices Kendrick to indiscriminately blow his wealth on "coupes" and "cars"—*get it all, you deserve it Kendrick*, Uncle Sam urges. Like a devil on his shoulder or Iago in Othello's ear, Uncle Sam attempts to goad the rapper into assured destruction, saying, "I'll Wesley Snipe your ass before thirty-five." Kendrick illustrates the catch-22 of sudden financial abundance and exposes that a materialist desire is the very thing that can get one caught up by the state, hence the title of the song: "Wesley's Theory"—a reference to actor Wesley Snipes who was imprisoned on charges of tax evasion. Wesley's name invokes a disturbing trend of black celebrities haunted by the government (Uncle Sam) for a failure to pay what, apparently, is owed: Lauryn Hill, MC Hammer, Richard Pryor, Chuck Berry, and Ronald Isley have all faced imprisonment on charges of tax evasion. We can look as far back as Marcus Garvey when citing federal taxes as a controlling tool and (over)extension of the state in the lives of black celebrities. If we also consider the long history of unfair contracts, denied publishing credits, and minimized royalty checks within the music industry, the exploitation of black creativity by controlling white institutions and individuals is unconscionable. In foreboding harmony, "Wesley's Theory" closes with a swelling chorus of women who climactically declare, "Tax man comin'! Tax man comin'!"

This Dick Ain't Free

Free jazz, free verse, free movement—all of these modes of freedom are questioned and destabilized on the track "For Free? (Interlude)." What critics have called "free verse" sound, I call a variation of hardbop, a closely related subgenre of jazz with a deep blues belly that arose in the late 1950s and 1960s. Critics note that, in its complexity, bebop can be understood as the recovery of black sounding methods from the sanitized, commercialized cool jazz trend of the post–Second World War era. As scholar Mark Anthony Neal describes, "Bebop emerges partly, as a conscious attempt on the part of black musicians to remove black musical expression from the clasps of an often indifferent & exploiting marketplace."[8] In this way, the sound that carries Kendrick's poetry is already coded in capitalist critique. The spoken word tracks that punctuate *Butterfly* infuse raucous energy and scathing commentary, pointing an accusatory finger at all who consume the material. I'm interested in the ways that Kendrick's movement from rapping—patterned rhyming over a beat—to what's recognized as performance poetry ("spoken word")—a stream of consciousness akin to free verse jazz—indicates his deepening embrace of anti-capitalist values.

In "For Free?" America (the nation) is anthropomorphized, made into a living, talking character, and she is anything but beautiful. America is imagined as a sassy and demanding woman who belittles and emasculates the protagonist. "Fuck you, motherfucker, you a hoe-ass nigga . . . you ain't shit," begins a breathless tirade aimed to dimmish the rapper. She demands new, brand name clothing and luxury hair extensions ("that Brazilian wavy 28-inch") before dismissing him entirely, saying, "My other nigga is on, you off." She degrades the protagonist and measures his worthiness in regard to his capacity to materially and sexually satisfy her desires. She emphasizes that he is, after all, replaceable.

Kendrick responds to America with his own mutinous, oppositional barrage. He is defiant—knowing his value and refusing to be turned into a trick, he asserts, "this dick ain't free," a memorable punctuating refrain. Kendrick's flow is associative, spiraling, aggressive, and unforgiving. Consider, for instance, this tight triplet that propels forward through image, sound, and political desire.

I need forty acres and mule, not a forty ounce and pit bull. Bullshit! Matador Matador . . . / Had the door knockin', let 'em in, who's that? Genital's best friend. This dick ain't free!

Kendrick demands heretofore unfulfilled reparations, *forty acres and a mule*, that date back to the Civil War and the emancipation of enslaved Africans. From this demand for justice uncoils a playful yet deadly accurate linkage of images. Forty acres is flipped to a *forty ounce*; mule is rhymed with *pit bull*; pit bull disperses into an image of a rushing bull (*matador, matador*) and a dismissal (*Bullshit*) of central social problems: the association of black people with deviance (alcohol, vicious animals) and the unconsummated promises of full, equitable citizenship. In direct address to America, he localizes his continued dehumanization to enslavement origins, reminding her of her role in demarking human flesh as property to be bought and sold, a receipt of purchase, an owned good. This notion of persistence despite dehumanization carries over as the speaker reflects upon survival strategies cultivated among black people who made magic with "leftovers and raw meat," at once invoking the diets of enslaved black communities and the "making something from nothing" attitude of a resilient people.

As the poem unfolds, listeners come to understand that America has been imagined as a sex worker. If the figure of Uncle Sam is the pimp, then, in this poem, America is his hoe, a woman who exists in transactional relation to the speaker. He laments, "Pity the fool that made the pretty you in prosper," a line where exquisite alliteration animates America's shallow nature. She is a woman who proffers and profits from her good looks, and the speaker recognizes that participants who succumb to her demands are foolish and easily seduced. I find it significant that Kendrick subverts the typical pimp-hoe dynamic held up in the tradition of West Coast rap carved by rappers like Ice-T, E-40, Sugafree, DJ Quik, Snoop Dogg, Dru Down, and Mac Dre. Instead of the rapper gaining power as a hustler who traffics in sexualizing women, here, the rapper himself is the subject in jeopardy of being tricked out and exploited by an avaricious woman. While I'll have more to say about this pimp-hoe dynamic in the next section of this chapter, here I focus on the rapper's boisterous, hypermasculine bravado that edges on the border of unhinged.

Kendrick's obsessive return to his penis is haunting when considered alongside against the history conjured. Listeners are confronted with the ways that black men were sexually abused during slavery, forced to mate, evaluated by penis size, called bucks and brutes by slave masters. Upon Emancipation in the United States a campaign to label black men as licentious, lustful, uncontrollable rapists became the justification for brutal extrajudicial lynching. Sometimes black corpses were mutilated after the burning or the hanging, penises castrated by obsessive mobs. The speaker's focus on male genitalia speaks to the historical fetishizing of black men who are projected as hypersexual and lustful in the collective American imagination—at once desired and feared. Kendrick testifies to his feeling "dormant, dusted, doomed, disgusted" in the wake of America's mistreatment and still maintains a defiant, oppositional tone.

The accompanying music video is the artist's most surreal and playful within his growing visual oeuvre. Directed by Joe Weil of PsychoFilms (longtime collaborators for Black Hippy crew visuals), the music video builds upon themes of materialism and exploitation explored in Kendrick's hurtling free verse. The role of America is played by model Hikeah Kareem, and she is fabulous as she struts through a mansion in a lacy black teddy and robe, yelling demands for a "baller ass, boss ass nigga" into a cellphone. Suddenly, Kendrick appears looking neurotic with bugged-out eyes and spasmic body movements, startling her. The dynamic between the intrusive Kendrick and the dripped-out woman who is trying to go about her day is comical. He intrudes upon America as she moves about her mansion performing mundane tasks. He is impish and unrelenting, moving and mouthing in exaggerated, exuberant ways insisting, "this dick ain't free." America retreats from Kendrick's dogged pursuit but finds him inescapable as the two play a cat and mouse game around the spacious grounds of the luxurious estate.

A Sambo figurine flashes on the screen and, at times, superimposes Kendrick's form. The Sambo, a relic of white racist propaganda that depicts crude images of exaggerated, yielding black figures, reinforces the idea that historical trauma continues to impact those living today and appears in the most unexpected places. When America measures the rapper's manhood in regard to wealth-based success, she upholds reductive notions of black masculinity and black femininity that are rooted in antiblack beliefs. On one level, the dialogic relationship between America and Kendrick presents painful commentary about the strained relationship between black women and their counterparts, one that is mediated by a lust for materialism that disrupts any chance for real intimacy. On another level, he dramatizes the relationship of the black entertainer to the exploitative institution—an alluring but demanding "bitch" who continually mis-recognizes and mis-categorizes the black performer. When Kendrick rattles off a vulgar litany in the first performance piece on the album, "For Free? (Interlude)," he is of the tradition of black power satirists whose manipulation of language highlights the vulgarity of the US superstructure. As scholar Margot Natalie Crawford explores in her book *Black Post-Blackness*, satire and humor are crucial elements of Black Arts Movement descendants invested in black worldmaking.

Kendrick's repetition of "ain't free" comes to carry multiple valences over the course of the song. "Ain't free" as in, one must pay capital to access any part of me—*this show ain't free to watch*. "Ain't free" as in, I am bounded, limited, restrained—*this body ain't free to move*. "Ain't free" as in, the condition of black life carries an intrinsic cost, a psychological price of the ticket—*this mind ain't free*. With each repeated utterance, the question mark of the track's title (For Free?) reverberates into an ambiguous, unstable, and unresolvable notion of freedom for the black male subject. The speaker's paradoxical free/not-free condition is the thematic center of a dense and nuanced poem where meaning accrues, building atop itself until all of it threatens to crumble under the pressure of the verse's closing couplet:

> Oh, America, you bad bitch, I picked cotton that made you rich
> And *now* my dick ain't free (emphasis mine)

Kendrick's subtle change of the refrain to "and *now* this dick ain't free" highlights the connection between an oppressive slave past (then) and a contemporary condition of debased black manhood (now). America continues to pimp black folks and get filthy rich in the process. And tellingly, she gets the last word in this heated exchange, declaring, "I'mma get my Uncle Sam to fuck you up. You ain't no king." America is a bully who calls in her pimp Uncle Sam for protection. In the first part of *Butterfly*'s narrative, America and her pimp are presented as omnipotent and unvanquishable forces.

And if the vocal delivery of "For Free?" is feverishly mad, the music video gestures toward a sense of lightness and peace. After the wild chase scene, the video closes with many Kendricks who simultaneously occupy the same frame. Kendrick trims hedges in the background. He reads a book underneath a tree in the foreground. He drinks champagne over a beautiful brunch spread. He plays a game of one-on-one basketball with himself on one side of the scene and a game of croquet on the other. In one shot we are presented with the idea that there are many iterations of the rapper, and none of these duplicates are in agony or experiencing mania. Each enjoys a Zen-like, joyful state. Perhaps it is possible for the fractured self who is pulled in so many directions at once to find peace and pleasure in the midst of a demanding and demoralizing world.

"For Sale? (Interlude)"

In title, "For Sale? (Interlude)" functions as the sister-track to "For Free? (Interlude)." Each questions the intrinsic and market valuation of the black entertainer, and each track dramatizes the big temptations that come with big money.

"For Sale?" reveals that Kendrick's new level of success is laden with existential traps that threaten to corrupt the rapper's spiritual and ethical intentions. These hazards are strikingly different from the landmines dotting the mad city from which the good kid escaped. This new sphere contains new rules, new dangers, and new lessons to be learned.

"For Sale?" introduces a new character who, like America the sex worker and Uncle Sam the tax man, is another antagonist in Kendrick's harrowing narrative: Lucifer. Within *To Pimp a Butterfly*, Lucifer manifests as "Lucy," a corrupting temptress who echoes the character of Sherane in the rapper's earlier work. Elsewhere I discuss hip-hop's proclivity for positioning the black woman as metaphor. She becomes a cipher to establish masculinity, and in Kendrick's work, she is the embodiment of vices and temptation that threaten to tear him asunder. Characters like Sherane (the girlfriend) America (the sex worker) and Lucy (the corrupting temptress) fulfill the same function. Here I examine how Kendrick participates in the P-Funk tradition by borrowing specific tropes and symbols of the genre, updating them for a new and contemporary message. To do so, I turn to Funkadelic's 1972 album *America Eats Its Young*, an understudied yet obvious precursor to *Butterfly*.

Panned as "messy," too-long, and "schizophrenic"[9] by contemporaneous critics, *America Eats Its Young* explores a wide range of themes and styles. The double-LP feels unbounded and exploratory, like an album on the brink of possibility but ultimately missing its mark. Notably, *America Eats Its Young* is the first Funkadelic album to welcome brothers Bootsy and Catfish Collins, recruited from James Brown's band. Along with Bernie Worrell's orchestral string arrangements and the use of electric guitars, there are beautiful and interesting moments that emerge. As I return to *America Eats Its Young* nearly fifty years after its release, I think the ambitious project possesses its own kind of brilliance in regard to black musical production.

Perhaps Kendrick shares this musical opinion of the album's value because the resonance between *To Pimp a Butterfly* and *America Eats Its Young*, particularly the political commentary of each, is palpable. Kendrick's insistence that *we gon' be alright* reverberates in harmony with Funkadelic's proclamation that *everybody's going to make it this time*. The advice of Kendrick's grandmother that *shit don't change until you get up and wash yo ass, nigga* reminds me of Funkadelic's refrain *if you don't like the effects then don't produce the cause.* And, although none of the tracks of Funkadelic's *America Eats Its Young* contain the searing rage of "The Blacker the Berry," the band provides a stinging class critique of America, one that illuminates the anti-materialist ethos Kendrick adopts and adapts from earlier radical musicianship.

Most important to this study are two Funkadelic songs: "Miss Lucifer's Love" and the album's title track "America Eats Its Young." On both tracks, the antagonists America and Lucifer are personified as debauched women who become the embodied metaphor against which the black masculine self is defined. "America Eats Its Young" is a slow-tempo, guitar-led R&B ballad (of sorts) that features a lone spoken verse delivered by down-pitched male voice (very similar to the voice heard on "Wesley's Theory"). The track opens with the shivers of a woman overlaying a man's quiet groans. The woman's shivers give way to moans, and it becomes increasingly clear that we are listening to the sounds of a sensual sex act. The deep voice begins to drowsily speak, depicting America as "A luscious bitch" who is as destructive as she is attractive. She is one who "like all hoes / is jealous of her own shadow" and who "sacrifice[s] the great grandsons and daughters." She spreads ruin across generations:

> By sucking their brain until their ability to think was amputated
> By pimping their instincts until they were fat, horny, and strung-out
> In her neurotic attempt to be queen of the universe

The depiction of America as an insatiable, wrathful manipulator of men is an image adopted and remade by Kendrick. But the similarities between the two records do not stop there. Funkadelic and Kendrick both transform Lucifer into a female character, one who is a corrupting temptress for black subjects who dare shape themselves on their own accord.

"Miss Lucifer's Love" is a standout track on Funkadelic's admittedly uneven *America Eats Its Young*. Fuzzy Haskins and Clinton are at their best over the heavy, heaving rock-soul ballad that sounds like a combination of Black Sabbath and the Temptations. They croon, "Miss Lucifer's love / She's the devil and I like it . . . / Ooh, her love is so exciting." The track builds with trembling anticipation as the protagonist awaits Miss Lucifer's destructive love, confessing that "When she come / I'll drink from her unholy fountain." Finally, the song explodes into searing guitar licks.

In Christian mythos, Lucifer is the fallen angel who, upon being cast out of Heaven, expels his energy promoting lies and propagating chaos in ultimate opposition to God. He is the personification of evil and the bearer of supreme darkness. In Parliament's adaptation of the figure, Lucifer controls and manipulates via sex, and the subject is all too willing to be undone in her presence. In Kendrick's re-gendering of Lucifer as Lucy, she is the embodiment of evils encountered with fame—and the rapper has the frame of mind to be wary. Miss Lucifer and Lucy promise certain ruin in the lives of Clinton and his P-Funk inheritor. What begins as sweet promises ("Lucy gon' fill your pockets / Lucy gon' move your momma outta Compton") quickly turns alarming as she becomes controlling and pompous. So assured is she that the speaker will succumb to temptation that she makes farce of the spiritual journey relayed on Kendrick's breakthrough debut record (*good kid, m.A.A.d city*). She reveals that she has been an omnipresent factor, commenting that "All your life I've watched you," an admission that sounds more like a threat of merciless surveillance and enmeshment rather than loving care. Lucy claims dominion over the rapper who, despite his sharp sensibilities, seems to have little control over the pacing and trajectory of his life. The rapper's vocal register drops to reveal Lucy's mutable nature—vocal modulation within Lucy's persona indicates a shape-shifting capacity to be both alluring and repulsive, sweet and bitter. She predicts his inevitable downfall because "at the end of the day you'll pursue me."

Funk expert Francesca T. Royster writes, "P-Funk through its sound, lyrics and use of theatricality on and off stage, makes room for a more exploratory and decentered notion of black male identity."[10] P-Funk calls for listeners to carve a life for themselves outside of racial-capitalism's dehumanizing processes, to reevaluate normative ways of thinking and being. The goal is to free your mind so your ass will follow, to dance your way outside of constrictions, to strive for higher planes of knowledge and enactable power. When one considers Kendrick's boundary-breaking, enlightenment seeking impulse and multiplicity of voices he crafts across narrative-centric albums, Parliament-Funkadelic's cosmology is germinal. When Kendrick depicts America and Lucy as conniving, despoiling women, he extends a P-Funk tradition of gendering and sexualizing abstract ideas to illuminate power dynamics that impact and impair black men. Kendrick draws on the power of P-Funk to assert an alternative, transgressive persona in the contemporary rap landscape—a persona where masculinity does not rely upon material consumption to bolster one's sense of value but, rather, builds strength from a wellspring of faith. Attempts to balance ugly representations of female antagonists early in the album appear when the artist comes to new planes of consciousness.

If These Walls Could Talk

Some might mistake "These Walls" for a simple song about the pleasures of sex. Quite literally, the track begins with whispered word "Sex!" followed by the sounds of a woman's moans (note the P-Funk echo). A groaning saxophone mimics her voice, and it is unclear whether this call and response signals pleasure, pain, or a combination of both—the woman's comingled bliss-blues sets the tone for the narrative that unfolds. In some respects, "These Walls" is about pleasure; however, it is not a love song. What appears to be a sexy-sweet tune with a bounce made for roller skating turns tragically dark. Structurally, the rapper deploys one of his favorite rap tools to great effect—he introduces a shattering narrative climax that requires listeners to rewind and playback for magnified meaning.

Bilal brings a Prince vibe to the track, crooning, "I love it when I'm in it" over a mid-tempo danceable groove and the scene is simple: A woman is out on the town and looking to "exercise her right to work it out." It is the night of her birthday and, as singer Anna Wise affirms on the bridge, "Everyone deserves a night to play." She and Kendrick meet for a night of sexual pleasure, and their time together is risky ("no life jacket," meaning, no condom) and racy ("interrogated every nook and cranny"). The relationship reveals itself to be laced with questionable motivations by both participants. For the woman, sex is a method of assuaging deep loneliness; temporary physical pleasure is a way to "relieve tension." For Kendrick, casual and risky sexual activity is a method for coping, what he calls a "defense mechanism" within his own life. Each partner finds in the other a fleeting fulfillment for a gnawing void.

Gradually, sensual metaphors give way to psychological tensions, and the image of walls closing conveys the sensation of a mounting panic attack. "Walls feeling like they ready to close in / I suffocate, then catch my second wind," says the protagonist. Panting breath collapses orgasmic pleasure and constricting fear, suggesting the two—pleasure and fear—are intertwined. Kendrick builds upon the theme of social and spiritual constriction and the word "walls" gathers layered nuance over the course of the song. Vaginal walls, emotional walls, prison walls—these barriers are sexual, emotional, and physical and, at times, indistinguishably intertwined.

In the third verse, the twist drops: the rapper has targeted this woman. This is retribution. Kendrick has targeted and seduced the lover of a prisoner serving a life sentence in the shooting death of his friend. This woman has a child with the shooter and in the rapper's calculation, Kendrick has spoiled the strongest connection to a life defined outside of punishment for the prisoner. Not only does the murderer have to finish life behind bars, but he has been "cuckolded," a term I use to highlight the sense of ownership both men possess in regard to the woman's bodies and desires. For Kendrick, "retaliation is strong," and though the rapper should be enjoying his new stage of fame, he is preoccupied with settling old scores. This is an ugly, harmful side of our transcendent and moral prophet of the hood.[11] He takes advantage of a single mother's trauma to temporarily fill an absence with hollow and mean-spirited sex. Out of his own grief, he succumbs to dark desires and, in his retaliation, not only commits harm against an unsuspecting woman but executes psychological torture upon an imprisoned man. The song closes with Kendrick yearning for the walls (the prison walls and her vaginal walls) to taunt and torment the prisoner into eternity. There is no closure, no healing for the open wounds exposed in the track.

"These Walls" is critical to the album's narrative development because the track centers imprisonment as a motivating impulse of Kendrick's work. In a song that doubles as a metaphor for good pussy, Kendrick highlights the tortuous and dehumanizing nature of prisons. Though delivered in an untraditional method, we come to feel how imprisonment is a form of intense suppression where one is disappeared from civil society, stripped of agency, and severed from people who endow one with the sense of sovereign humanity. Although liberation is nowhere near achieved by any member of the dark trio described, the song depicts the depth of depravity that can be cultivated within an *institutionalized* environment. By the song's close, we expand our notion of whom the prisoner is—the life sentencer, the woman, and Kendrick himself in all of his vindictive spite are each imprisoned within a noxious web spun by grief, violence, and state punishment.

Institutionalized

You know they got me trapped in this prison of seclusion
—*Tupac Shakur*

The primary impulse of *Butterfly* is liberating love—a type of love for brethren that is rigorous, self-reflective, uplifting, and pedagogical. It is a love that teaches and reaches out. He says, "I make my music basically for people in the prison system and kids in college because they got nothing but time. . . . I want it to be an actual course that you could take and live with."[12] *Butterfly* centers carceral language and "institutionalization" comes to take on varied meanings as the track's narrative develops. For Kendrick, one can be *institutionalized* within the criminal justice system, within a devitalized neighborhood, within politics, within a demanding music industry, and most importantly to Kendrick's artistic intentions, within one's own limited, flawed notion of self. The track "Institutionalized" begins with a confession:

> I'm trapped inside the ghetto and I ain't proud to admit it
> Institutionalized, I keep running back for a visit—Hold up

The recursive stutter ("Hold up. Get it back.") of the song's introduction conveys the feeling of being hopelessly mired, unable to move beyond one's current position. And when Kendrick revises his meditation on institutionalization, the sentiment is supremely bleak: He declares, "Institutionalized, I could still kill me a nigga." The rapper articulates a mindset forged in poverty where home is a place of dangerous belonging that lures the speaker back into deadly patterns. The echo of Tupac's "Trapped," a song that testifies to the killing rage that accrues in the institutionalized individual, reverberates in his protégé. The first single of his debut album *2Pacalypse Now*, "Trapped," tells the story of a "young black male" who is harassed and abused by police, so much so that he makes the calculated decision to die by police bullets rather than continue a living death *in this prison of seclusion*. Kendrick veers away from this grim tale with a hazy set of *zoom, zoom, zoom*'s reminiscent of Afrika Bambaataa's "Planet Rock" to deliver his meditative introspection on morality.

The two verses that comprise "Institutionalized" illuminate a protagonist coming into awareness about his new social position and all of the attendant burdens, pleasures, and responsibilities embedded within that position. He learns that financial success and global popularity do not necessitate happiness, let alone freedom. He learns that it is hard to merge beloved alliances and newfound social circles, the hood and Hollywood. He is a star who stands squarely with one foot in each world, and his role within the industry shifts, so too does his role within his clique. A classic boom bap percussion drives an ensemble of keyboards, violin, cello, and most vividly, a careening clarinet that captures the sharp-edged precarity within Kendrick's voice. He confesses that "I'm probably just way too loyal," thereby encouraging or dismissing bad behavior from his crew. He elaborates,

> Truthfully all of 'em spoiled, usually you're never charged
> But something came over you once I took you to the fuckin BET Awards
> You looking at artists like harvests

When the protagonist brings his crew to the BET Awards, they hatch plots for "snatching jewelry" and "harvest[ing]" riches of the elite. They resort to instincts carved in the hood, and we hear the frustration in Kendrick's voice. Legendary West Coast rapper Ice-T speaks of the difficulty of leaving a ghettocentric mindset behind, saying, "Once you grow up in the inner city, it's always gonna be in you. . . . Your points of reference are still going to be the same, but you'll have the opportunity to begin the breakdown of that aggressive, survivalist mentality."[13] Kendrick corroborates Ice-T's O.G. insights and laments the ways that lust and greed distract from greater purpose, saying, "Dream only a dream if work don't follow it." For Kendrick the dream must be coupled with a hard work ethic in order to manifest and actualize *success*, a concept the rapper will trouble.

Kendrick flips the point of view to deliver the second verse from the perspective of the friend who considers jacking attendees for jewels. He declares, "My defense mechanism tell me to get him quickly because he got it," disclosing a ruthless self-interested spirit. The friend-persona evinces a Robin-Hood spirit, saying, "Remember steal from the rich and giving it back to the poor? / Well, that's me at these fucking BET Awards." He is unable to sit in the moment and take in the beauty of blossoming from Compton to this special immersion within black excellence. Instead, a poverty mentality urges the industry newcomer to seek materialism and to hustle would-be kinfolk in the world of black artistry. "Institutionalized" doesn't provide resolution by moving beyond the two contrasting perspectives of the rapper and his homie. There is no moral proffered. Instead of a third verse, we encounter an outro performed by West Coast pioneer Snoop Dogg who delivers a singsong bridge reminiscent of Slick Rick's "Children's Story" and unforgettable 1980s classic.

That Snoop mimics the unmistakable cadence of Slick Rick's "Children's Story" is significant. When he debuted on "Deep Cover" with Dr. Dre in 1992, Snoop stunned listeners with his ultra-smooth, cascading flow that was quickly likened to Slick Rick the Ruler. Moreover, Snoop showed critical awareness of and reverence for his inheritance by covering Slick's "La Di Da Di" (updated to "Lodi Dodi") on his 1993 solo debut *Doggystyle*. Thus, Snoop showcases an aesthetic sampling that carries with it an enduring past narrative.

In "Children's Story," Slick Rick recites a fable about a boy who is schooled in the art of armed robbery, "misled by another little boy." The fable is delivered as an adventurously tragic bedtime story—the easily influenced protagonist becomes intoxicated by quick money and escalates, robbing "another and another and a sister and her brother" at gunpoint until he sticks up the wrong person: an undercover police officer. The rest of the song unfolds in a vivid chase scene as the kid turns tail to run for his life. Listeners feel the frenzied desperation of the teenager who has run out of luck as he dashes into pedestrians and a dope fiend, wrecks a stolen car in a high-speed chase, and then takes a pregnant woman as hostage. "Deep in his heart, he knew he was wrong," so he releases the hostage before, finally, dropping the gun in surrender. The song ends in foreseeable tragedy as Slick Rick rhymes:

> He was only seventeen, in a madman's dream
> The cops shot the kid, I still hear him scream[14]

"Children's Story" takes place "once upon time not long ago" such that this morality tale of teenage recklessness and desperation in the face of police menace remains timeless, is always happening *not long ago*. When Snoop takes on Slick Rick's flow in Kendrick's bridge, he carries the time-honored story with him. He quickens the couplet rhyme scheme to relay the brief tale of a "little nigga" in the "divine" city of "Westside Compton"—Piru territory—who is "dazed and confused / talented but living under the neighborhood ruse." Snoop warns of a ghettocentric mindset where one "can't take the hood out the homie" or, in other words, cannot adjust to existence outside of a ghetto environment. Slick Rick's own unfortunate experience with guns and imprisonment coupled with Snoop's felonious background augment the precarity of caterpillars that have yet flown as butterflies from reckless environments.

With Snoop's short six-line bridge (composed by Kendrick), the song ends and, like many others on the album, offers no solution, only the space for meditation about complicated ideas, images, and sounds. "Institutionalized" considers the limits of emancipation from a ghettocentric, survivalist mentality and the rapper will go on to complicate this notion by considering the incongruousness of black talent and institutions coded by whiteness.

Loving u Is Complicated

The track "u" is *Butterfly*'s most grim and offers distressing insight into dark recesses of the artist's tortured soul. While on a career high, Kendrick reaches an emotional bottom where the accumulating impact of grief, guilt, and depression threatens to pull the rapper asunder. Screaming, cursing, and crying on the track, Kendrick presents a man in the midst of a break. Producer MixedbyAli (Derek Ali) recalls the sudden and sullen way in which the track came together, saying, "[The] session for 'u' was very uncomfortable. [Lamar] wrote it in the booth. The mic was on and I could hear him walking back and forth and having these super angry vocals. Then he'd start recording with the lights off and it was super emotional. I never asked what got into him that day."[15]

The visual component of the track—a short film titled "God Is Gangsta" that combines "u" with "For Sale? (Interlude)"—dramatizes the scenario: the rapper is drunk and distraught, alone in a hotel room and facing his inner demons. He rakes himself over the coals, cataloging a list of failures in regard to loved ones while away from home— his teenage sister's pregnancy and the murder of his little nephew weigh heavily on his conscience, evoking feelings of "blame" and "shame." The repetition of "still," a word that becomes the fulcrum of the verse, emphasizes how problems and feelings that are repressed can and will resurface. No matter the stage of one's success, you might *still* fall to pieces, *still* find yourself fracturing under the weight of trauma and responsibility. Kendrick reckons with the hypocrisy of being hailed a rapper of moral and ethical conviction who yet, in his estimation, is "irresponsible, selfish, in denial" and "can't help it."

"u" offers insight into the deterioration of an artist pressurized by new fame and old affiliations. This version of Kendrick is demoralized and defeated: "you fucking failure—you ain't no leader!" he screams at himself. As the distraught speaker continues to explore the dark parts of his interior, it becomes increasingly clear that an overwhelming sense of fear pervades his psyche—fear of exposure; fear of disappointment; fear of accountability; fear of untimely, tragic demise. He threatens himself with potential exposure, saying,

I know your secrets—don't let me tell them to the world
About that shit you thinking and that time you . . .
(*gulp*), I'm bout to hurl

The act of suicide is gestured toward but left unspoken as the
rapper dramatizes his devolution into paralyzing guilt.

Kendrick's deprecating self-examination reveals how
immobility and the inability to positively reach beloveds
can inspire spiraling and crippling depression. This song
reminds me of how feelings of helplessness can creep up on
the striving black individual who dares to imagine themself
free, who dares to imagine they've risen above whatever
weighty state they've survived. The reality is that no matter
our success, no matter our wealth and accomplishments, we
might suddenly and swiftly be paralyzed by realities of loss,
death, and inequity. I am also reminded of the impossible
choices that success-seeking individuals face—"You even
Facetimed instead of a hospital visit / Guess you thought he'd
recover well," Kendrick recalls. When the speaker confesses
throughout the song that "loving you is complicated"—a
refrain repurposed from the one and only, Tupac Shakur[16]—
we come to understand that "you" is the self and the other. It
is hard to love one's flawed, imperfect self, and it is likewise
difficult to love one's flawed, imperfect kin—family, friends,
fans—to whom one is fatefully and fatally connected.

As hip-hop culture continues to mature, topics of
mental health and wellness have been increasingly probed
and embraced. Artists like Kanye West, Kid Cudi, Tech
N9ne, Mac Miller, and Eminem have crafted highly visible
public personas that make art of neuroses, rehabilitation

processes, and psychiatric disorders. And, of course, the catalog of classic rap songs that provide insight into the emotional and social world of the neurotic or breaking individual is expansive.[17] *To Pimp a Butterfly* contributes to the discourse on mental health by thinking through the ways that wealth is alienating, transitory, burdensome, and dangerously maddening for the black artist. Kendrick models to listeners that the quest for enlightenment is an extended process that brings up nasty feelings that disrupt one's sense of stability but that also opens possibilities in surprising, incalculable ways. On mental health and fame Kendrick says,

> What I do is for a greater purpose and we all need money and things like that to survive, but the energy around some of these spaces, it can draw you into a crazy place. And I've seen and heard some of the greats go out because of it. And I'm saying this right now to let everyone know, it's real and you have to be mentally steady 100 percent in order to keep doing it at a high level and still maintain your sanity.[18]

On Macklemore and Cultural Appropriation

Elvis was a hero to most, but he never meant shit to me
Straight up racist that sucker was —*Public Enemy*[19]

Black life has become increasingly public in the post-civil rights landscape and art, as opposed to politics, is the dominant vehicle for that accessibility. Currently, blackness appears to be at maximum proliferation—hip-hop pervades all genres in sound and style; black representation across media from film to drama is in the midst of renaissance; the subject of black life mattering or not mattering remains a prevalent debate. Paradoxically, the heightened visibility of blackness in public life becomes the selfsame logic for renewed repression and the refusal of humanity. As a multibillion dollar industry where real wealth can be achieved, rap music finds itself increasingly invested in material consumption. And given the market's inescapability, it is no wonder that rap culture embraces material excess and pleasure as primary objectives. What is more recognizable or more revered in the United States than the accumulation of riches and beautiful women? *To Pimp a Butterfly* offers insight into the market's stranglehold on black expression and voices the vexed nature of the artist who attempts to escape. But first, a little history.

Since the popularity of 1920s race records when blues music and blues philosophy was first captured and distributed by music companies, the agency of black artists has been impacted by segregating and exploitative market forces. Historically, the popular black artist has had to navigate the expectations and demands of polarized white and black audiences—those racial lines are increasingly blurred in the globally connected, streaming age we find ourselves. However, interdependent relationships between the black artist, consumers, and the record industry still exist, and sometimes, profitability is at odds with artistic voice—sanitization, censorship, and caricaturizing are possible costs for the black artist when making music for mass consumption. The very nature of black art in the United States, at once produced from a marginal place yet centered within that society as a primary fount of musical innovation, is contradictory. Historically, this structural component of entertainment industries perpetuates a black/white dichotomy that is consistently measured, tested, recalibrated, and yet, maintained.

The American musical landscape is comprised of predictable patterns of innovation and appropriation whereby black sounds become filtered through whiteness, so much so that the original cultural essence of the originating sound is minimized. Emergent sounds produced in sovereign spaces like juke joints, rent parties, and slave quarters have historically remained, for a period, inaccessible to and untouched by outsiders until discovered, packaged, and sold by white investors. For instance, during the 1930s swing era, white bands imitated and adapted black sounds, whitewashing a genre innovated by black musicians whose marginalized positions and sensibilities shaped the genre. In the postwar period when rebellious young whites discovered the gut-bucket sounds of rhythm and blues, the term "rock and roll" came to be used for white artists like Bill Haley, Elvis Presley, and Buddy Holly who adapted blues sound. During the 1970s, disco was embraced as a "raceless" and watered-down variation of soul. Today we hear hip-hop's distinctive African-derived rhythms, expressions, and stylings in genres labeled "white" from country to pop to rock. Undeniably, hip-hop influences from the use of samplers and drum machines to rap vocal techniques run through every existent genre.

The late scholar Perry A. Hall describes the dynamics of black cultural contributions to popular culture as a *dialectical* process, one where "diffusion" and "appropriation" exist in interdependent relationship.[20] Historically, innovation within the black musical tradition experiences an initial stage of revulsion before entering the marketplace. This revulsion is spurred by the unrecognizability of the innovation—strange, eccentric, and yet unheard, this new form is labeled and understood as potentially threatening to the social order. Innovations like the blues, jazz, funk, and hip-hop have all experienced brief, formative moments of autonomy that is feared by a public with purchasing power. Next, black innovation undergoes acceptance and proliferation—that proliferation eventually reaches a point of streamlining and absorption. The result is that any oppositional, radical essence of the original innovation is evacuated—black sound is bereft of its kinetic, transformational potential. All secular black American musical forms have experienced this commodifying process. Blues, jazz, funk, hip-hop—each of these innovations has undergone recognizable patterns of diffusion and appropriation.

Celebrating fifty years of cultural contributions, hip-hop culture is, arguably, at a height of diffusion. The last decade of rap has seen the increased prominence of white musicians charting Top 40 lists, a barometer that may reveal more about the youth-driven demographics and attitudes of disposability of pop music's profit schema rather than the Billboard's ability to measure social impact. Macklemore closed 2013 with the top spot in year-end numbers. Miming and mining black women's performances, Iggy Azalea accelerated to the top of the charts in 2014. Mac Miller, Logic, G-Eazy, Lil' Pump, Post Malone, Jack Harlow, not to mention Eminem's decorated twenty-year career attest to the cultural proliferation of rap and changes within the genre. Certainly, at the time of Kendrick's entrance into popular culture, hip-hop appeared positioned at a critical moment of whitening and diffusion.

Hypercommodification of black musical innovation has far-reaching consequences. Cultural innovators are often left bereft of economic and industry rewards as white businessmen and imitators adapt black musical forms into palatable productions—a few experience belated recognition. I am thinking of women like Florence Price and Margaret Bonds, two classical composers who, many decades after their deaths, are beginning to see their works made available to the public. As black originators are diminished and erased, singular black musicians are rendered exceptional, leaving behind a skewed and incomplete archive. Moreover, the extraction of black aesthetic innovation reinforces malicious racial ideologies. Hall writes, "the Black human beings whose collective living experiences most consistently contribute innovative impulses to the music of the wider culture continue as despised, feared, rejected symbols of undesirability."[21] In other words, as black cultural production is cultivated and even celebrated in the popular sphere, and although white listeners and audiences have been attracted to the aesthetic sensibilities of black people, little true engagement with the political content of black musical production is engaged and, tellingly, the notion of the "Other" is maintained and reified.

In response to processes of voyeurism and appropriation, underground countercultures form to move away from assimilationist, middle-class industry standards and back toward the folk roots of black expression. Thus, bebop emerges as an innovative response to the sanitized big bands of the swing era. Funk emerges as an innovative response to the integrationist aesthetics of soul and "raceless" objective of disco. In this way, one may recognize the formation of hip-hop as a return to cultural roots and reclaiming of musical autonomy, one that rebels against respectable and easily legible characteristics of the rhythm and blues generation before it. These experimental and avant-garde strains like bebop, funk, and hip-hop that arise in the invisible underground, in the fugitive spaces farthest outside of the market's reach, share emphasis on layered polyrhythm, kinesthetics, and improvisation; they arise as expressions of authenticity and reclamation.

For black popular artists, the market is inescapable and changing dynamics influence cultural production. Kendrick bears witness to the rage that accrues when the artist desires freedom within a controlling global market. This is a rare perspective in hip-hop and in sentiment, I am reminded of the incomparable Prince who spearheaded a historic protest against Warner Brothers Records for control of his music. In fact, he was supposed to feature on *To Pimp a Butterfly*. Kendrick remembers, "Prince heard the record, loved the record and the concept of the record got us to talking. We got to a point where we were just talking in the studio and the more time that passed we realized we weren't recording anything. We just ran out of time, it's as simple as that."[22] It is an extraordinary endeavor to imagine the conversation that unfolded between these two great avant-garde artists and the creation that could have been made. Prince might have simply provided the hook for "Complexion," but we all know how time stops and possibilities unfold in collaborative sessions with the legendary musician.

In 2014 Kendrick was nominated for seven Grammy Awards, a barometer that attests to the breakthrough success of *good kid, m.A.A.d city*. He was expected to win big and celebrate induction into a new echelon of fame. However, the rapper took home no awards that year—he was shut out entirely, losing three of the biggest categories including "Best New Artist," "Best Rap Performance," and "Best Rap Album" to Macklemore & Ryan Lewis, a white hip-hop duo from Seattle, Washington, who no longer perform together and whose careers have since diminished. It was a travesty. Everyone knew that Kendrick deserved to win, including Macklemore himself who first messaged Kendrick privately, then posted his private message to Instagram for the public to see.

> You got robbed. I wanted you to win. You should have. It's weird and sucks that I robbed you. I was gonna say that during my speech and I froze. Anyway, you know what it is. Congrats on this year and your music. Appreciate you as an artist and as a friend.[23]

This public posting of a private message meant to be a cleansing salve only served to confirm the layers of antiblack logic embedded within the industry and its participants. At the interpersonal level, Macklemore attempted to distance himself from culpability by claiming allyship. Macklemore could have spoken in the moment, made private amends, refused the award to make a historic stand, done any number of things that would have displayed true allyship in the music industry. But he chose to publicize a private message and then book radio spots to further discuss the debacle. *Anyway, we know what it is.*

At the structural level, the debacle dredged up old wounds because the Recording Academy has a long history of failing to acknowledge and award the range of black talent that propels the music industry, especially rap music. The snubbing of Kendrick rang back to the 1989 boycott of the ceremony led by DJ Jazzy Jeff & the Fresh Prince when the Academy announced they would not televise rap categories. After Beyoncé's masterpiece *Lemonade* (an album I also write about)[24] was similarly overshadowed in favor of Beck's *Morning Phase*, the hashtag #GrammysSoWhite circulated social media spheres, and it was clear that something needed to change. In 2018, the Recording Academy responded by adding an additional 900 voting members to its selection panel and avowing a commitment to diversity. As if making amends for previous sins, Kendrick's next album, *To Pimp a Butterfly*, would be tremendously awarded by the Academy with a cornucopia of trophies in 2016 (see Chapter 3: Love).

The Blacker the Berry

The colonized subject discovers reality and transforms
it through his praxis, his deployment of violence and his
agenda for liberation. —*Frantz Fanon*[25]

Kendrick said very little about Macklemore's public display of white guilt. Robbed of the crown in 2014, he would pen his frustration about the plight of the black artist within entertainment. If anything, his track "The Blacker the Berry"—a verbal slaughter—is the reply. On this track, Kendrick rages outward. Written years earlier in the wake of Trayvon Martin's murder and revived for *Butterfly*, the rapper speaks directly to the figure of the white supremacist who appears in the shadows of the song's lyrical landscape. He repeatedly asks, "You hate me, don't you?" and points an accusatory finger, saying, "your plan is to terminate my culture" and make "[me] irrelevant to society." Kendrick's vocal texture is of gravel and grit, full of boiling anger as he confronts his oppressor and identifies how, representationally and economically, white supremacy replicates. Where the rapper confronts the racist as an obvious antagonist, he also confronts an American public who readily consumes his art, thus challenging listeners to examine their own position within a racist and classist matrix. The artist critiques (white) fans who consume rap music because they consider it a portal to the distant, forbidden hood—"You never liked us anyway, fuck your friendship, I meant it." In this double-speak, he condemns the explicit racist and the complicit, unaware neoliberal who feigns friendship yet upholds the killing structures that diminish black life and black artistry. Not enough attention has been paid to Kendrick's ability to double-speak—his ability to address distinctive, sometimes contradictory audiences within a singular breath or verse or song or album-long narrative.

In stunning fashion, the rapper rapidly sifts through the accumulated detritus of what revolutionary theorist Frantz

Fanon calls the black *imago*[26]—the preconceived ideas of blackness that box-in and name the subject as "black" before the subject even has the chance to name himself. Kendrick takes the slew of negative associations attached to the black male head on when he proudly proclaims, "My hair is nappy, my dick is big, my nose is round and wide." Kendrick articulates how black men have been methodically characterized as threatening specters within the American racial imagination—rapists with monstrous penises; cold killers deserving of prison. In response, Kendrick unleashes a barrage of images that reclaim the power and sovereignty of the black individual: "I'm African, I'm African-American / I'm black as the moon, heritage of a small village."

"The Blacker the Berry" profoundly spins around the black/white color line that structures US social and political life. The lyrics emphasize how blackness and whiteness exist in dialectical relationship to one another such that the notion of blackness as vulgar, excessive, and sinful is upheld in opposition to the dominant notion that whiteness is of rightness and reason. The rapper emphasizes how these ideas are fictions—merely the creation of a nation aimed to designate heroes and villains in the grand theater of citizenship. Kendrick positions himself as the feared, uncontainable outlaw figure who, with embodied rage, exposes how stereotyped notions of blackness are always and already circulating, circumscribing the imagination of dreamers in profound ways. He is the lawless, avenging creature of America's nightmare, product of the nation's own merciless greed: "You sabotage my community, making a killing / You made me a killer, emancipation of a real nigga."

"The Blacker the Berry" addresses the fact that race is and has always been a chief structural component of American life, a fact that shapes outlooks and limits outcomes. The thick patois of the pre-chorus highlights shared diasporic experiences and names chattel slavery as the originating, still-open wound.

I said they treat me like a slave, cah' me black
Woi, we feel a whole heap of pain, cah' we black
And man a say they put me inna chains, cah' we black

Enslavement is the indelible condition that continues to shape black life and all that we have gained and lost in the aftermath—Jim Crow and civil rights victories; mass incarceration and increased militarism—all of it is the residual hauntings of colonialism and slavery. The rapper addresses the paradoxical position of the modern black person who, once an object to be owned, struggles in the wake of emancipation with actualizing full, uncompromised subjectivity. For the rap artist who strives for success on the global market, material excess replicates dynamics of bondage. "Gold chains" and "the whip" collapse the weapons of slavery with the emblems of luxury. The bridge indicates that the modern black artist is enchained and hurting, and at the root of this hurt is antiblackness.

Although the boldness and truth-telling aspects of "The Blacker the Berry" were widely celebrated, Kendrick faced harsh rebuke for the single's closing couplet. Phrased as a rhetorical question, the couplet was interpreted as damaging and disruptive to a building liberation movement. He asks,

So why did I weep when Trayvon Martin was in the street
When gangbanging make me kill a nigga blacker than me?

I am interested in how the naming of Trayvon Martin not only positions the rapper in movement discourse but localizes his inquiry in the territorializing nature of men. I am thinking about how the seventeen-year-old boy was pinpointed, stalked, and murdered by George Zimmerman for *looking out of place* in the Sanford, Florida, gated community. Kendrick juxtaposes this territorialization to that of gangs who commit violence along boundary lines. I also find it valuable to question the possibility of working in the name of black liberation while committing harm within one's community. This broader question of harm seems urgent for a movement threatened to be discredited with accusations of opportunism, money mismanagement, the exploitation of death.

Two dominant criticisms arose in response to the rapper's incendiary close—that Kendrick first, embraced (regressive) respectability politics and second, reinforced false right-wing conspiracies about "black-on-black" crime. Criticism toward the rapper was further enflamed when, asked to comment on the Ferguson Uprising, Kendrick responded, "What happened to [Michael Brown] should've never happened. Never. But when we don't have respect for ourselves, how do we expect them to respect us? It starts from within. Don't start with just a rally, don't start from looting—it starts from within."[27] *To Pimp a Butterfly* reveals a narrative sculpted with the express intent to lessen the harm of gang violence in Compton—to imagine some kind of unity beyond territorialism and murderous rage—and the unruly, disquieting nature of "The Blacker the Berry" reflects the difficulty of that worldmaking. In response to critics of the closing couplet, the rapper reminded naysayers of the first-persona, personal narrative and his experiences in Compton, saying, "Preachy? I missed that because the majority of the album is me talking about my faults."[28] Kendrick emphasizes that his process of self-interrogation and self-discovery, a journey that he exposes for the benefit of listeners, is not only transformational but, at times, tortuously dark. Certainly, the controversy surrounding the track's closing lines speak to the ever-contested terrain of Black Lives Matter (BLM) who, like all progressive movements, engage in self-scrutiny and recalibration in the pursuit of justice.

Released as the album's second single, "The Blacker the Berry" is a five-minute lyrical assault against the intractability of white supremacist racism and serves as a dynamic counterpart to the artist's mobilizing first single, "i," discussed at the end of this book. Swinging between intimacy and conflict, love and hatred, the two singles act as foils to one another to construct the argument that the black condition is one of psychological fragmentation; it is a state of racialized "schizophrenia"—a term the rapper employs several times throughout "The Blacker the Berry." Theorist LaMarr Jurelle Bruce argues that within "The Blacker the Berry" Kendrick performs as a "sadistic" and "pyromaniacal" persona who activates schizophrenia to wrestle with antiblackness and death.[29] When the rapper begins "The Blacker the Berry" with an image of fire and destruction, I hear the psyche of an individual who, like myself, is compelled by the memory of black uprising and in our fiery contemporary moment of protest, uprising, and insurrection, experiences flashes of what bell hooks calls *a killing rage*. hooks writes that "Until this culture can acknowledge the pathology of white supremacy, we will never create a cultural context wherein the madness of white racist hatred of blacks or the uncontrollable rage that surfaces as a response to that madness can be investigated, critically studied, and understood."[30] Where Kendrick mobilizes madness to spotlight the enduring and debilitating nature of antiblackness, he also validates the rage that erupts in response to that malignancy.

2

Spirit

Indeed, to go back in any historical (or emotional) line of ascent in Black music leads us inevitably to religion, i.e. spirit worship. This phenomenon is always at the root in Black art, the worship of spirit—or at least the summoning of or by such a force.
—*Amiri Baraka*[1]

The chapter thinks through Tupac Shakur's influence on Kendrick Lamar's artistic values, narrowly, and hip-hop culture, broadly. In many ways, *To Pimp a Butterfly* unfolds as an intimate letter to the icon, one that reveals his indebtedness to and divergence away from Tupac's philosophies. I discuss Tupac's often misunderstood THUGLIFE worldview and his contradictory yet generative presence-in-absence. I chart the subtle and explicit ways that Kendrick writes and performs as heir apparent, articulating his own liberationist philosophy in the process.

****

To Pimp a Butterfly dropped exactly twenty years (and one day) after Tupac's 1996 album *All Eyez on Me* and, as fans know, little is coincidence in Kendrick's world. He openly discusses his fanaticism of Tupac, studying his lyrics and life with the intensity of a devoted scholar. Overt and subtle references to the rapper's work abound in his music. Earlier songs like "HiiiPower," "Keisha's Song," and "Poetic Justice" make explicit allusions to assorted 2Pac tracks and, composed as a meditative letter to his idol, *To Pimp a Butterfly* magnifies that scholarly devotion. Even Kendrick's origin story is steeped in Tupac as a guiding spectral figure. In a 2013 interview with *GQ* magazine, Lamar describes an eerie visitation from Tupac's ghost during a recording session, saying,

> I was coming for a late studio session, sleeping on Mom's couch. I'm 26 now—it wasn't that long ago. I remember being tired, tripping from the studio, lying down, and falling into a deep sleep and seeing a vision of Pac talking to me. Weirdest shit ever. I'm not huge on superstition and all that shit. That's what made it so crazy. It can make you go nuts. Hearing somebody that you looked up to for years saying *don't let the music die*, hearing it clear as day. Clear as day. Like he's right here. Just a silhouette.

Whether a true spiritual encounter, or a delirious dream wrought by a late-night work session, or a manifestation of internal ponderings—or some strange combination of all these things—Tupac's spectral visitation marks a turning point in Kendrick's career. Thereafter he adopts the professional duty to move beyond typical tropes of "money, hos, clothes, [and] drinkin'" to instead speak to and for poor, dispossessed communities. He steps into a leadership role, and from this formative moment onward, Kendrick's musical and moral compass is fixed toward liberation. In the rapper's words, he reflects that "The overall theme (for me personally) for this album is really "leadership." How can I use it? With money and with celebrity, how can I pimp it? Can I pimp it negatively, or can I pimp it in a positive way?"[2]

Tupac embodied the freedom-dreams of wanting black boys and the precariousness of engendering those dreams. When he spilled rage, thrusting both middle fingers in the air, spitting at the camera, shouting "Fuck the world!," for a short time he was hip-hop's impervious and indestructible ambassador—a modern outlaw the likes of Stagger Lee. With pretty eyes and wounded heart, a constellation of twenty-six tattoos over lithe muscles, Tupac offered the post-soul generation struggling in the wake of a crumbling Second Reconstruction the power of embodied rebellion, however brief. This was the man-child borne of Black Panther Party blood who survived death several times over: he arrived whole and healthy although his mother fought for one egg and a glass of milk each day to nourish her unborn son while incarcerated; he lived to boast about the confrontation and exchange of gunshots with two racist police officers in Atlanta; he won a settlement from the Oakland Police Department after they profiled, beat, and falsely jailed him; he appeared in court bandaged and dispirited—but alive—after taking four bullets, including one to the head, the night previous; *and* he managed to beat two felony raps in just eight weeks. Now twenty years gone, sculptors of hip-hop history have magnified the swift ascent and dulled the slow smothering of Tupac's brightly burning star.

Although he catapulted to infamy before the age of the internet, Tupac's rebellious mythos circulated in public culture in what one might call a *viral* fashion. As Nicole R. Fleetwood writes, "Racial iconicity hinges on a relationship between veneration and denigration,"[3] and certainly Tupac, who was eloquent, intrepid, socially engaged, and a crossover celebrity, negotiated the line between alluring and threatening. Both loved and feared, he moved through the world with a deep recognition of his body's layered significations, inking THUGLIFE across his chiseled abdomen in ironic defiance. Named after the Incan monarch and revolutionary Túpac Amaru who led an Indigenous uprising against Spanish colonial forces, it seemed fated the artist would shake up the world on behalf of the oppressed. As Quincy Jones once stated, "Tupac was America's worst nightmare." The rapper understood the demands placed upon his art—he was masterful precisely *because* he grasped the power of couching emancipatory rhetoric within street warrior performance. However, he publicly battled for moral balance and clarity when under the pressure of the public's fracturing gaze.

Certainly, Tupac was a host of paradoxes, advocating for uplift and self-determination on the one hand and glorifying dangerous street mentalities on the other. He offered audiences songs of racial uplift ("Keep Ya Head Up") and racial despair ("They Don't Give a Fuck About Us"); loving proto-feminism ("Do For Love") and vehement misogynoir ("Wonda Why They Call U Bitch"); boastful thuggery ("Hit Em Up") and introspective intellectualism ("So Many Tears"). As scholar Michael P. Jefferies explains, "the mechanics of hip-hop allow for conflict and contestation, even within bounded commodities. Songs and performances, in addition to being polyphonic, and often polytextual, are poly-ideological."[4] Where Tupac was defiance and militant-edge, he was also soft, sad, conflicted, and destined to die far too soon. In some ways it was a miracle that he made it to twenty-five—a tragedy that his potential was never fully rendered.

By the time bullets riddled his passenger side door—cutting into tissue and organ so severely that exploratory surgery, a removed lung, and heavy prayer could not save him—Tupac produced a tremendous opus in the nine years preceding his 1996 assassination. Seven films. Five albums. A book's worth of poetry. Hip-hop's first-ever double LP certified 9x platinum. Undoubtedly, he was a gifted and ambitious artist. He was the embodiment of both the Black Power generation's ambitions and the brutal unraveling of those dreams—he was the Panther Party's prince, and as rhetorician Gwendolyn D. Pough notes in her essay, "Seeds and Legacies," "a lot of people thought that Tupac was going to be the next great Black leader."[5] Having risen from poverty to prosperity while under intense public scrutiny, the rapper's demeanor changed remarkably as his once buoyant and charming intellectualism gave way to paranoia, boisterousness, and flagrant materialism. Because the rapper used the page and recording booth to pour out what he was feeling from moment to moment (as Kendrick does), and because his life story highlights the strained relationship between black Americans and a punishing state (as Kendrick does), I find Tupac himself and his body of work to remain a special archive that captures aspects of black life and black world making at the turn of the twenty-first century. Kendrick, too, regards Tupac as a vital epistemological source.

THUGLIFE

I see you blackboy
bent towards destruction watching
for death with tight eyes—*Sonia Sanchez*[6]

Endowed with material and spiritual lessons from the Black Panther Party (BPP), Tupac showed no fear in challenging police forces—for instance, while living in Oakland, he was known to videotape officers interacting with citizens, a counter-surveillance technique for documenting and checking misconduct. In the month before the release of *2Pacalypse Now*, Tupac filed a $10 million brutality lawsuit against the Oakland Police Department, alleging physical assault by the police officers who ticketed him for jaywalking. The beating occurred after police officers did not believe that his real name was "Tupac Shakur" when prompted to identify himself. Tellingly, the department settled with the rapper for more than $40,000. Two years later while touring in Atlanta, Tupac experienced another potentially deadly encounter with law enforcement officers. As the details of the story unfolded, it became clear that once again the officers in question abused their authority and acted out of line with unnecessary force during a road rage incident. To make matters worse, the police officers were intoxicated. Tupac shot the first officer in the stomach and the second in the buttocks. After some months of litigation, all charges were dropped; however, his estate was eventually ordered to pay some $200,000 in civil court.

That Tupac managed to escape death and evade prison sentences in explosive encounters with white policemen was shocking. Certainly, these events have aided in the construction of his mythological cultural status. These encounters also reveal the rapper's willingness to confront a lawless state in defense of the human right to live unmolested and unharmed. Together with his BPP inheritance, Tupac's numerous negative experiences with law enforcement and his subsequent incarceration for nine months at the Clinton Correctional Facility, a maximum-security prison in upstate New York, informed his political motivations and larger critique of American value systems. Away from marijuana, alcohol, and his entourage, Tupac experienced clarity while incarcerated. He wrote screenplays, music, and the initial drafts of a policy platform called the "Code of THUGLIFE." Like the Nation of Islam and BPP which sought to rehabilitate street hustlers like pimps, gang members, and drug dealers, Tupac developed a training program for ghetto youth to channel energies and street knowledge for collective nation-building. Tupac appropriated and remixed the policy-driven strategies of his BPP inheritance to codify a list of universal rules that would seize control of black neighborhoods and, in turn, generate autonomy for folks confined to decaying urban cities. Though many scholars have addressed the political intentions of THUGLIFE, Seneca Vaught has produced the most comprehensive examination of its principals, insisting that Tupac's philosophy should be considered, "a policy proposal" because it directly addresses the ideologies buttressing social laws and "outlines a particular strategy for decision-making in the Black community."[7]

For Tupac, gang activity did not have to be so bloody and destructive—no more stray bullets at playgrounds and parties; no more unwarranted misery for ordinary folks. Some of THUGLIFEs tenets included no slinging (drug dealing) crack cocaine to children or pregnant women; protection of elders and civilians; the use of diplomats to settle disputes between gangs; and markedly, to "Control the Hood" because "the Boys in Blue [the police] don't run nothing, we do." Ultimately, Tupac was concerned with instilling self-respect, reducing intercommunal crime, and sustaining harmonious order within black neighborhoods. He imagined a utopian space where black civilians no longer cower to domineering policemen nor battle senseless violence. Tupac re-imagined gang members as street warriors who would protect citizens, especially those considered vulnerable like children, women, and elders; they would also provide for their respective neighborhoods by netting income from illicit economies like drug dealing. THUGLIFE envisioned black cities free from punishment and castigation and instead controlled through community-run informal agreements and management systems. His vision bears a strong resemblance to discourse about abolition fomented by #Black Lives Matter organizing.

When one contrasts Tupac's THUGLIFE to the BPP Ten Point Platform, a striking dissimilarity in tone and scope emerges. For instance, the first credo of Tupac's philosophy is particularly disturbing: "All new Jacks to the game must know a) he's going to get rich, b) he's going to jail, and c) he's going to die." Where members of the BPP implicitly accepted imprisonment and death in the name of liberation as grim possibilities given the fierce federal campaign to extinguish the group's efforts, THUGLIFE embraces death not as a distant possibility in the name of moral righteousness or structural change but as an inevitable outcome for any street soldier. Unlike the Ten Point Platform that demands structural change in which African Americans have equal opportunity in the economic sector—simply worded, "We want full employment for our people."—THUGLIFE delegitimizes normative economic avenues and instead names street hustling, primarily drug dealing, as the central source of income in black neighborhoods. Tupac never seemed to acknowledge the basic hypocrisy of peddling poison to the very civilians he vowed to protect for he seemed to myopically regard the pusherman as the linchpin of free enterprise.

Tupac traveled to ghettoes across America ministering to gang leaders and teaching the lofty, if contradictory philosophies of THUGLIFE. After the Los Angeles Uprising of 1992, the Bloods and Crips, notoriously deadly rivals, signed the Code, vowing to develop community programs and quell violence crippling black Los Angeles. During his time in prison, Tupac continued to refine and develop THUGLIFE and conceived of implementing the Code in chocolate cities across the United States. However, his murder precluded this possibility. THUGLIFE was not only the striking tattoo stretched prominently over Tupac's chiseled abdomen; it was the archival evidence of the rapper's political imagination—an imagination that developed early. I want to suggest that scholars and fans have done a deep disservice to the inheritors of hip-hop by mis-remembering the full scope of Tupac's political vision and aspirations. Recovering the expanse of Tupac's grassroots activism from childhood to his death, Dr. Karin L. Stanford insists that "Tupac Shakur should be regarded as a cultural worker."[8] Stanford traces Tupac's long engagement with activist work, noting that he participated in his first public outcry at the tender age of seven when attending a New York rally where he delivered a speech. Additionally, Tupac catalyzed a schoolwide boycott during his elementary years in support of his teacher who was fired due to financial cutbacks. Although the boycott would prove ineffectual in securing his teacher's return, young Tupac learned early the power of community-organized protest.

Tupac's grassroots philosophies blossomed while attending the Baltimore School of Performing Arts where he auditioned and was accepted to major in acting. It was at this performing arts school where he wrote his first rap—a eulogy for a friend murdered by gun violence. Organizing campaigns for AIDS awareness, leading the Young Communist League, and creating politically oriented spoken word performances during his high school years, Tupac was not just a boy with lofty ideas—he, indeed, was a cultural worker who embodied the spirit of his BPP family by putting into action black nationalist philosophy that serves the people. As Stanford writes,

> The willingness of the BPP members to assert themselves into the daily struggles of people, without adherence to ideological purity, demonstrated their commitment to uplifting the quality of life for Black people. Similarly, Tupac supported Black nationhood and wealth redistribution as long-term solutions, while at the same time, he worked to address immediate problems.[9]

Certainly, there was a severe generational shift between post-soul ghetto youth and their Black Power parentage; however, Tupac Shakur illuminates how the "post" is just that—derived from what and who came before yet fundamentally different in composition. That Tupac was raised by a motley of Black Power-affiliated kinfolk and that he deliberately chose to surround himself with these same individuals during his period of fame speaks to his moral compass and the base from which he began to build his own political theory. Tupac's mother was BPP member Afeni Shakur, and he regarded political prisoner and former Revolutionary Action movement member Dr. Mutulu Shakur as his figurative and spiritual father.[10] Additionally, he considered infamous Black Liberation Army (BLA) member Assata Shakur as an aunty. Watani Tyehimba, leader of the New Afrikan People's Organization (NAPO), served as Tupac's business manager and mentor, along with his godfather Geronimo Ji-Jaga Pratt, former minister of defense for the Los Angeles chapter of the BPP. Tupac was surrounded by highly respected black nationalists whose lessons in freedom-fighting guided his decision making, artistic sensibility, and public utterances.

No matter how far Tupac seemed to veer from the noble righteousness of his BPP inheritance, he consistently espoused and enacted black nationalist strategies within the constricted space of the music industry. For instance, throughout his career, he formed several groups that advocated for fiscal and ideological autonomy—even his controversial move to Death Row Records was inspired by the desire for financial and aesthetic independence.[11] In 1991, Tupac formed the Underground Railroad, a collective of uplift-minded MCs from around the country. In an interview with legendary Bay Area radio DJ Davey D, Tupac explains his motivation:

The concept behind this [Underground Railroad] is the same concept behind Harriet Tubman, to get my brothers who might be into drug dealing or whatever it is that's illegal or who are disenfranchised by today's society—I want to get them back into [*sic*] by turning them onto music. It could be R&B, hip-hop or pop, as long as I can get them involved. While I'm doing that, I'm teaching them to find a love for themselves so they can love others and do the same thing we did for them to others.[12]

This vision that Tupac held early in his career reminds me of LA rapper artists like the late Nipsey Hustle who practiced this form of reaching back and lifting up. Kendrick, too, quietly gives back to his community, funding programs for Compton's school district behind the scenes, among other philanthropic endeavors. Tupac would go on to form several rap groups that combined rap's therapeutic rawness and Black Power's community engagement; however, his dreamy plans to blend art and politics into one powerful medium never reached fruition. For instance, in the months before his death, Tupac talked of organizing the One Nation project—an album that would unite East and West Coast groups and, hopefully, would put a rest to the bitter rivalry. Unfortunately, he was murdered in Las Vegas before this possibility. Coupled with murder of Bad Boy Records rival The Notorious B.I.G. just seven months later, Tupac's death did more to quell hip-hop's murderous tide than any album ever could.

Revisiting Tupac's past with an eye toward his long engagement with grassroots organizing, community-building, and public performances of politicism recovers the tremendous threat to power the rapper posed.[13] Where and who would Tupac be if he had lived to 2017? How might his political thought concerning liberation and nation-building have progressed as he continued to study, create, and reinvent himself? These questions continue to haunt hip-hop and very well should haunt America's national conscience. As Joan Morgan wrote in her seminal autocritography, "It is criminal that the only space our society provided for the late Tupac Shakur to examine the pain, confusion, drug addiction and fear that led to his arrest and his eventual assassination was in a prison cell."[14]

California Love

I'm not saying I'm gonna change the world, but I guarantee that I will spark the brain that will change the world.
—*Tupac Shakur*[15]

The logics of hip-hop have always depended on the firm allegiance to place, a notion that rappers of the gangster era exploited to the point of several rappers' deaths during hip-hop's bloody civil war.[16] Tupac was unique for a popular rapper in that, unable to mark one specific location as home, he was unmoored. He shuttled back and forth between Brooklyn and Harlem before moving to Baltimore. He ultimately relocated to the Bay Area (Marin City) with his mother after reluctantly quitting the Baltimore School of Performing Arts before his final year, a memory he disappointingly recalled at times. In a 1994 interview with Kevin Powell for *Vibe*, the rapper confessed, "My major thing growing up was I couldn't fit in. Because I was from everywhere, I didn't have no buddies that I grew up with. Every time I had to go to a new apartment, I had to reinvent myself. . . . Hell, I felt like my life could be destroyed at any moment."[17] Indeed, Tupac was always searching for stability and permanency, from without and within. He learned early the art of acting as a survival tactic—reimagining and presenting oneself according to the environment. One sees this adaptability in his relationship with Death Row Records when he plugged into LA's gang-affiliated music scene and managed to win the hearts of black residents in the city penning classic odes like "California Love" and "To Live & Die in L.A."

Kendrick recalls seeing his idol for the "California Love" video shoot in 1995, saying, "When Tupac was here [Compton] and I saw him as a 9-year-old, I think that was the birth of what I'm doing today. From the moment that he passed I knew the things he was saying would eventually be carried on through someone else. But I was too young to know that I would be the one doing it."[18] Nearly twenty years later when Kendrick filmed his own music video for "King Kunta," he memorialized Tupac Shakur and paid homage to a greater rap tradition through performance. The music video for "King Kunta" celebrates the ordinary exquisiteness of blackness within Compton and is described as a "day in the life" by Director X. Shot at locations around Compton; the video foregrounds iconic West Coast visuals—classic lowriders, neighborhood locals lining the sidewalks of Palm-tree lined Compton streets, dancing women, a good time all around. The video's square aspect ratio and golden filters imbue scenes with a bright sense of nostalgia; a vintage vibe coats scenes of every day fun. One sees the act of memorialization most as Kendrick performs from the roof of the Compton Fashion Center, a landmark site in hip-hop culture.

Informally referred to as the Compton Swap Meet by locals, the site holds considerable hip-hop history. Besides selling goods that directly benefited black families, up and coming artists came to the swap meet to sell and exchange mixtapes and 12-inch singles. These tapes couldn't be purchased elsewhere making the Fashion Center one important nodal point in LA's underground rap scene. In a now-infamous 1989 episode of *Yo! MTV Raps*, NWA spotlighted the swap meet as a destination site during a tour of Compton, bringing visibility to hip-hop voyeurs outside of Los Angeles. By the time Tupac and Dre filmed there in 1995, the site was iconic. Just weeks after filming "King Kunta," the Compton Swap Meet was replaced by a (gigantic) Wal-Mart, signal of changing city and a rap era's demise. As Director X remembers, "We went there really just to keep with the West vibe. I mean we knew that Wal-Mart bought it, but once we got there and saw it's actually closed it became this kind of big going away party."[19]

As the visuals pay homage to West Coast legends, so too does the sound of "King Kunta," undeniably the *nastiest* g-funk groove on *To Pimp a Butterfly* and, perhaps, in Kendrick's growing oeuvre. Produced by Soundwav under Kendrick's direction to amplify the rhythm, the song's architecture embeds a genealogy of LA g-funk artists. Soundwav recalls,

When we first did "King Kunta," the beat was the jazziest thing ever with pretty flutes. Kendrick said he liked it but to "make it nasty." He referenced a DJ Quik record with Mausberg ["Get Nekkid"] and he told me what to do with it. I added different drums to it, simplified it, got Thundercat on the bass, and it was a wrap.[20]

Beyond the Mausberg / Quik reference, Kendrick also incorporates Ahmad's "We Want the Funk." Mausberg and Ahmad are (regionally) well-known rappers whose respective singles made a huge impact on music in southern California. Personally, Ahmad's "Back in the Day" from his 1993 self-titled album *changed my entire life*. I listened to the record on tape via Walkman through terrible headphones and memorized every word, suffering sanction for repeating the word "Nigga" aloud all throughout the house at eight years old. Ahmad was one of the first rap artists whose vivid use of language and rhyme brought a lively story to life in my mind. After the success of "Back in the Day," he went on to graduate from Long Beach City College as valedictorian and earn a PhD in Social Welfare from Stanford. On the other side of the spectrum, Mausberg (DJ Quik's talented protégé) suffered a different fate. He was shot and killed at just twenty-one years old—his debut album *Non Fiction* released posthumously. Together, Ahmad and Mausberg are representative of the stark and clashing possibilities facing brilliant kids in postindustrial Los Angeles. "King Kunta" embeds these histories of funk, fatality, and flight within a boastful jam about dominating the rap game.

We Gon' Be Alright

Ask Rodney, Latasha, and many more
It's been going on for years, there's plenty more
—*Tupac Shakur*[21]

In his raps, Tupac elegized the victims whose deaths, in part, compelled the 1992 Los Angeles Uprising. He was one of the only rappers to continually lift up the name of Latasha Harlins, a young black girl who was fatally shot in the head by a Korean store owner for allegedly stealing an orange juice. While Latasha's story was eclipsed by Rodney King's controversial footage in national media, in Los Angeles her murder and the killer's acquittal were incendiary sparks for historic uprising. Tupac illuminates the relationship between antiblack violence and uprising. Following the lines quoted above, he goes on to state:

> They ask me, "When will the violence cease?"
> When your troops stop shooting niggas down on the streets.

The rapper predicted ongoing tension between law enforcement and black citizens if no systematic changes were made to alleviate suffering and, in his utterances, voiced the spirit of Black Lives Matter decades prior to the movement's inception. Kendrick Lamar has taken to heart his idol's role in fusing fractions among territorialized and terrorized neighborhoods in his THUGLIFE policy, and, on wax, he considers the stakes of carrying on that legacy for himself.

Butterfly's standout single, "Alright," is the first black anthem of the twenty-first century to be recognized as a freedom song cohered to a freedom movement—the largest social movement in the history of the United States.[22] The year *To Pimp a Butterfly* dropped, police killed at least 1,152 civilians, and when Kendrick's anthem debuted in early summer, it gave protestors the energy to be louder than ever.[23] For me, "Alright" is inextricable from my mourning and organizing work for Sandra Bland who died under mysterious circumstances in a Waller County, Texas jail cell. The year had been rough. 2014 saw the solidification of BLM as a national movement after the murder of Mike Brown Jr. and the subsequent Ferguson Uprising. Early in 2015, footage of Natasha Mckenna, naked, bound and tasered to death by law enforcement officers, circulated the internet. Later that year, fifty-year-old Walter Scott was gunned down after fleeing a traffic stop in Charleston, South Carolina. In the same month, the neck of 25-year-old Freddie Gray was broken in the back of a police transport van, and he died from his injuries sparking days of fiery uprising in Baltimore. "Alright" became an instant anthem for a growing protest movement, soothing the pain of these terrible incidents and stoking flames of righteous rebellion.

When Kendrick penned "Alright," he may have had uplift on the mind but not necessarily protest. And the track itself held a strange history. Pharrell had the track, at least the foundations of the beat and melody of a nascent chorus by late 2013, a full year before Kendrick began writing to it. Some hip-hop heads may have heard rapper Fabolous's leaked version that circulated the internet—it is well known that Pharrell shopped around before finding a home with Kendrick who crafted the lyrics that would propel "Alright" to historic heights. Pharrell remembers, "That chorus I had for a while, like that structure, the feeling of that chorus—but then Kendrick recontextualized it."[24] Production by Pharrell shines—phantom keys intone a harmonized and airy *duh*,

duh, duh that progress in semitone before the heavy kick of booming bass drum kicks in. A skipping snare and light piano keys, coupled with the bright and wandering arc of Kamasi Washington's tenor saxophone, imbue the feeling of flight above the dark, roiling bottom. Journalist Jayson Greene notes that "Kendrick's voice has nearly failed him on 'Alright.' It's reduced to a scraping wheeze from too many shows, too many studios takes, too many verses, and you can nearly hear his throat closing protectively around his vocal cords. It gives his performance a ragged, desperate, strangely exultant edge."[25]

> Wouldn't you know we been hurt, been down before (nigga)
> When our pride was low, looking at the world like "where do we go?" (nigga)
> And we hate po-po, want to kill us dead in the streets fo sho (nigga)

Strikingly, "Alright" is the only track from the tremendously personal album that utilizes the communal *we*, indication that this chant is to be taken up by all listeners. The bridge captures the voice of a people who, in the words of Fannie Lou Hamer, are sick and tired of being sick and tired. Kendrick voices the desires of a people who have witnessed the consolidation of a police state and who yearn for an alternative world where black subjectivity is valued, where black aliveness is possible.[26] Kendrick centers police as a lawless force and the antagonizing problem in black life; they are forces who kill with precision (*for sure*) and for spectacle or sport (*for show*). The bridge closes with a mounting sense of urgency and a breathless line that lays bare the stakes:

"I'm at the preacher's door—my knees getting weak and my gun might blow but, we gon' be alright!" The rapper leaves room for throwback civil rights tactics that center pacifism (*the preachers door*) but also holds space for violent rebellion (*My gun might blow*). In Kendrick's worldmaking, both strategies are viable, urgent options for catalyzing change. The simple and infectious refrain *we gon be alright!* rings like an echoing battle cry that beckons all within ear range. The insistent and unadorned brevity of *we gon' be alright* makes the dream of freedom seem graspable and worth the continued fight.

Certainly, the anthem's viral nature was aided by the cinematic and enchanting music video that replicates the album cover in tone and texture. Scenes are shot in a high-contrast, silver-tinted achromic palette. Bright luminescence breaks through deep shadows and bright skies illuminate minimalist scenes of industrial sites—working-class environments like workshops, bridges, and factories are highlighted as the driving centers of a sprawling city. Like all of Kendrick's collaborators, director Colin Tilley reflects fondly upon Kendrick's hands-on technique and meticulous nature, saying, "I've never actually worked with an artist like Kendrick that wants to keep pushing the creative to a whole 'nother world. Every little detail matters to him."[27] The atmosphere is leaden and yet free, rebellious movement is celebrated. Death is omnipresent and yet a reality where black individuals are unkillable is imagined. Kendrick conceptualizes a video of contrasts that combats a contemporary condition of sorrow with vivid images of transcendent aliveness.

The video's narrative begins in conflict. Serene establishing shots of desolate city streets and industrial spaces are contrasted to the quick sequence of a man who is wrestled to the ground and handcuffed by a police officer. As he struggles to his feet and turns to run, the office pulls the handgun from the holster, aims down the barrel, and shoots. It is unclear if the bullet strikes its target because the frame suddenly changes to a dreamlike world. Instead of engaging in murderous gun battles, in this alternative dream world officers serve. Four policemen haul an entire car on their shoulders, as if bearing the rapper and his entourage in royal carriage. Boys and girls dance atop police cars; they dance in the streets; they dance in front of a tower of speakers—a wall of kinetic sound. All of it is rebellion and revelry in aliveness. Kendrick defies laws of gravity, nimbly floating through the air past Oakland and LA landscapes. He embodies the freedom of flight and provides audiences with the visual image of moving outside of constrictions.

Each of these images subverts power dynamics that would appear to be ossified in the United States. The cops who haul the vehicle that is both carriage and coffin are in positions of service, fulfilling an oath regularly negated in poor and black communities. The dancing children occupy space without threat of violence and are able to express joy in their sovereign, innovative movements. When Kendrick perches atop a traffic light in Downtown LA, the vital financial heart of the metropolis that lies just a few miles from South Central, he boasts victory in spaces where black men like himself were never meant to excel nor survive. In his flight, Kendrick is simultaneously earthly and otherworldly. He is superhero, prophet, and deliverer. Ruefully, he will also be made martyr.

Kendrick balances on a lamppost that lies high on a hill above Los Angeles. The atmosphere is serene, and Kendrick appears in calm control as he watches over the city. Children run up the path, pointing with glee to behold the rapper transmit his powerful message to the city below. A police officer, too, sets his sights on the perched rapper before shaping a gun with his fingers, pointing upward, and mouthing a silent "Pow!" He pulls the (metaphysical) trigger and a (material) bullet strikes the rapper, sending blood flying and his body hurtling to the ground. The scene of the crime is captured in agonizing slow motion. And though his limbs flail in attempt to break his fall, the rapper's face shows something akin to relief, perhaps acceptance, in his death descent. Just when the viewer has been made breathless having watched a liberated, soaring man felled by a bullet, Kendrick opens his eyes, gazes at the viewer, and *smiles*. The screen turns black indicating a sudden, startling end. The rapper's teasing smile is disquieting in a world where black women and men are regularly killed, especially in a year cited as one of the most violent in regard to police shootings of unarmed black people.[28] If we understand the video to take place in an imaginative space where the black individual is unkillable, then the persistent presence and murderous power of the police is anachronistic and unimaginative. Undoubtedly, Kendrick's performance of flight inspires a larger, pressing question—What does a black world look like where brutalizing police do not exist?

Although hip-hop has been speaking truth to power for nearly five decades and although the culture has produced a huge catalog of antiestablishment, politically astute songs, few singles have risen to the level of anthem. Musicologist Shana L. Redmond writes,

> Anthems demand something of their listeners. In performance they often occasion hands placed over hearts or standing at attention. Yet more than a physical gesture, anthems require subscription to a system of beliefs that stir and organize the receivers of the music. At its best this system inspires its listeners to believe that the circumstances or world around them can change for the better—that the vision of freedom represented in the song's lyrics and/or history are worth fighting for in the contemporary moment.[29]

In the post-soul, hip-hop age, Public Enemy's "Fight the Power" and NWA's "Fuck tha Police" stand as protest songs that have endured time and remain markers of communal consciousness-building. Although the messaging, tone, and instrumentality of Public Enemy and NWA's anthems diverge, Public Enemy and NWA emerge from environments where crack cocaine's public health crisis and the lawless nature of police forces in conjunction with widespread poverty made for austere militancy. "Fight the Power" encourages black underclass communities to fight in the political realm for their natural rights whereas "Fuck tha Police" endorses a physical clash between citizens and law enforcement. Both, however, attest to living in postindustrial wastelands amid citizens-turned-zombies by crack cocaine. Both name public urban spaces as the sites of contestation against the state's militarized, corrupt regime. Both question and destabilize the legitimacy and fortitude of white supremacy, but where Public Enemy advocates dismantling, NWA embraces extermination. Kendrick augments the legacy of rap anthems that attest to black life in a police state and inspire revolutionary thought on the part of the listener.

"Alright" garnered superlative praise from critical outlets such as *Rolling Stone* and *Pitchfork*, and the video was praised as a tour de force. More profoundly, "Alright" was adopted as the anthem for a generation of cultural workers who were and continue to be angry, exhausted, and bitterly hopeful. Of "Alright" the rapper reflects, "I'd say that's one of my greatest records because it gave these kids an actual voice and an actual practice to go out there and make a difference. They're going out and they're walking the walk and talking the talk whether it's inside their communities, whether it's inside their juvenile systems. They wanna make change."[30]

Resurrecting Tupac

There is no inheritance without the call to responsibility.
—*Jacques Derrida*[31]

Tupac is of the generation of black youth who bore witness to an astonishing and fearsome vanishing as the bodies of parents, cousins, friends, and lovers were quite literally ghosted—casualties of drugs, incarceration, AIDS, and gunshots. Since before his death-by-drive-by, Tupac has been speaking from beyond the grave. Steeled for the afterlife, songs like "I Wonder if Heaven Got a Ghetto," "Only God Can Judge Me," and "Death Around the Corner" reflect his resignation to depart this earth before thirty. No other rap artist in the history of hip-hop has anticipated, performed, and packaged his always-impending death to the extent of Tupac Shakur. Consider the song "So Many Tears" where the rapper confesses that "My every move is a calculated step to bring me closer / To embrace an early death, now there's nothing left." In Tupac's world, death was not something to be feared but an inevitable conclusion to rebel life. In his spectacularized engagement with the culture of death, even when alive, Tupac existed in a liminal space within an etherealized body that flirted with and exposed the limits of subjectivity.

In her work on the "queer art of death," scholar Sharon P. Holland notes that "some black performers have embraced the culture of death as a way to move their bodies out of space and into time."[32] Of a generation where 1 in 3 black men were marked for prison and boys prepaid for funeral ceremonies to save their families the worry and expense, Tupac's death-drive exposes and refuses a "universalizing" narrative that equates black youth with systematic extinction. Imagining afterlives where gangsters have been shown mercy and admitted into heaven into the Thug Mansion, the rapper's attempts to "move out of space and into time" through performances of death-as-art was a strategic, if nihilistic, method of disrupting fatal realities of abjection with projections of black immortality. *I wonder if heaven got a ghetto.*

Perhaps because in his queer performance of death-as-art he asked us to, participants in hip-hop culture have persistently attempted to resurrect Tupac. Remarkably, more material has been released after his death than during his lifetime. Coupled with the still-circulating legend of his Machiavellian-like staged death, the rapper's eleven posthumous album releases and numerous guest features, the Broadway play, young adult novels, and T-shirts bearing his face, the circulation of meme's, and his infamous Coachella hologram clearly indicate a collective desire to immortalize Tupac into an eternally speaking force. I build on Holland's work to probe a series of questions I find urgent. Why does Tupac's ghost continue to haunt us so? Why are we so hungry to fill the void that Tupac's death revealed? What is at stake in resurrecting Tupac?

Kendrick reevaluates Tupac's THUGLIFE philosophy to articulate a new political imagination—one adapted for our time and one that refuses the nihilism of self-immolation. This reappraisal is heard most clearly on *To Pimp a Butterfly*'s closing track "Mortal Man" where Lamar holds a conversation with Tupac's ghost. Using recovered audio footage from an unreleased interview, Lamar simulates an eerie conversation with the rebellious rapper who preaches about class rebellion and moral reckoning with that passionate, prescient, and affable voice of his—a voice we have been missing in hip-hop since his murder. The effect is chilling, so much so that I cried the first time I heard the song. I was stunned to hear Tupac's voice, so brilliant and so clear through my headphones, sounding impossibly alive. Clocking in at over twelve minutes, the song's closing position, length, and subject frame "Mortal Man" as the album's crown jewel. Moving through rap, g-funk, jazz, spoken word, poetry, and a conjuration, Lamar blends all the album's aesthetic genres into one powerful creation; thus, "Mortal Man" is a microcosm of *To Pimp a Butterfly*'s larger project, something akin to a thesis statement.

"Mortal Man" can be likened to Tupac's THUGLIFE platform in that the rapper endeavors to organize an underclass militia under a cohesive policy proposal delivered through music. This proposal unfolds though layers of sound as each aesthetic phase introduces a new aspect of a liberationist agenda. Beginning with song, Kendrick brazenly acknowledges and accepts the role of leader and prophet, using both terms to reference his cultural role. The rapper envisions his listeners as a militia and promises to "lead this army" despite human fragility—the "mistakes and depression" with which he struggles. Calling upon "the ghost of Mandela," the rapper examines his relationship to listeners to whom he directly speaks and questions their loyalty. He asks, "Do you believe in me?" and "Is your vow on lifetime?"

"Mortal Man" ponders a series of existential questions that meditate on the limits of the body and gravity of social responsibility. What are the possibilities for a man born in the postindustrial ghetto and catapulted to stardom to remain healthy in an industry as demanding as popular music? Moreover, what are the possibilities for morality within an industry that has historically required the spectacularizing of black bodies at, sometimes, the highest costs? "How many leaders you said you needed and left them for dead?" In conversation with Tupac's material and ideological ghosts, Kendrick aspires for a cultural immortality that is independent from tragic endings which have befallen so many icons of black struggle. He signifies a litany of cultural figures living at the nexus of pop culture and civil rights traditions including Nelson Mandela, Reverend Martin Luther King Jr., Huey Newton, Malcolm X, President John F. Kennedy Jr., and Reverend Jesse Jackson, Jackie Robinson, Michael Jackson, and even the biblical figure of Moses. Kendrick's ghostly cadre of leaders, those whom from his models his own liberationist aims, have been assassinated, scrutinized, criminalized, and propelled to mythological status in America's cultural imagination, leading the rapper to wonder, "Can you be immortalized without your life being expired?"

Tupac's silhouette hovers above Lamar's verses as he draws inward to articulate the contours of his own human vulnerability. Like Tupac, Lamar expresses the basic fear of expiring before reaching his full potential. Instead of a blaze of bullets that would cause physical death, Lamar catalogues a series of plausible occurrences that could result in his social death, like "If I'm tried in a court of law, if the industry cut me off / If the government want me dead, plant cocaine in my car." He introduces scenes familiar to black men in the public eye like drugs and court trials—entanglements that enveloped Tupac Shakur in the last stages of his life.

As the song portion of "Mortal Man" comes to a close, the titular poem which has heretofore slowly unfolded throughout the album is for the first time recited in its entirety. The poem picks up where *GKMC*'s narrative left off: on the heels of success, Kendrick reckons with sudden hypervisibility and spirals into "a deep depression." Like James Baldwin returning from Paris, only after leaving the city of Compton can Lamar find the clarity needed to organize and uplift. Having made it out alive while his kin continues to struggle in the mad city, the rapper confesses to "survivor's guilt." He reflects upon his experiences in the music industry and finds that although his environment has greatly altered with social mobility, conflict follows him and new battles waged in new sites of conflict remain rooted in race and class—what the rapper terms "apartheid and discrimination." Kendrick's poem reflects how the artist has begun to refine and refigure not only his philosophies and the language used to articulate those philosophies, but also his approach to implementing those beliefs into a substantive platform for community change. Like Tupac's THUGLIFE, Kendrick's poetic proposal targets a gang-identified underclass that through self- and communal-respect might cohere and thus build a self-controlled black nation. To explicate these policy-minded aims, Lamar sonically resurrects his idol Tupac Shakur by replicating the dreamlike visitation where this chapter began.

As the poem concludes, Lamar transitions to conversation with Tupac's ghost whose silhouetted presence finally materializes as a speaking specter. Lamar proceeds to hold an intimate exchange with his resurrected idol, asking him, "how would you say you've managed to keep your level of sanity?" and "what you think is the future for me and my generation today?" For nearly five minutes, Tupac enthusiastically responds with reflections about his faith and position as a black man in American society, ultimately advocating for armed self-defense in forging a new America that has been restructured from the bottom. He foretells of underclass rebellion where "the poor people is gonna open up this whole world and swallow up the rich people." Alluding to the events of 1992, he threatens that future uprisings by oppressed citizens will be more focused on their destruction: "I think niggas is tired of grabbin' shit out of the stores and next time it's a riot there's gonna be, like, uh, bloodshed for real! I don't think America know that . . . It's gonna be murder, you know what I'm saying, it's gonna be like Nat Turner 1831 up in this mothafucka." Tupac imagines something akin to a civil war for post-soul civilians and privileging his Panther inheritance—"it goes down my family tree"—conceives of (armed) resistance as an essential part of citizenship.

Kendrick Lamar's conjuration of Tupac Shakur is poignant because he not only captures the fullness of Tupac's organic intellectualism; in his sonic resurrection, he de-romanticizes Shakur by reckoning with the paradoxical nature of his mentor's ideologies and actions. Lamar responds to Tupac with his own articulation of freedom, one that departs from the violent visions of a race war, commenting that twenty years after his murder, "there's nothing but turmoil going on" and the "only hope that we kinda have left is music and vibrations." Lamar rejects Tupac's fatalistic death-drive and, instead, attempts to move *out of space and into time* through different means. For Lamar, there are alternative pathways for ghetto youth seeking transcendence—his metaphor of caterpillars destined to become butterflies highlights the possibilities for metamorphosis, transcendence, and vibrant aliveness.

Kendrick Lamar revealed that his acclaimed album was meant to have a different name: *To Pimp a Caterpillar.*

Acronymized, this shelved title would have been: T(u) PAC. In many ways, Lamar's sophomore release is a sort of musical manifesto, one that articulates a political ideology within and through Tupac Shakur. Stylistically, Kendrick has studied and absorbed the best aspects of his idol. Like Tupac, he raps with honesty, vulnerability, and urgency. Like Tupac, he is an avid storyteller whose confessional accounts traverse emotional, spiritual, and material registers. Like Tupac, he deploys personas to occupy various subjectivities and, in doing so, emphasizes a community of voices and experiences. Furthermore, like Tupac Shakur, he writes smart rhymes that attack systems of power. But where Tupac often strayed from his cultural undertakings to uplift and organize a struggling people, ultimately succumbing to his death-drive by various means, Kendrick Lamar holds righteously steadfast and challenges some of Tupac's most troubling characteristics including gangsterism, nihilism, drugs, and misogyny. He represents a new type of g-funk folk hero for the #BlackLivesMatter age and beyond.

3

Love

We are put on Earth to love.
—*Kendrick Lamar*[1]

This third and closing chapter examines the significance of *To Pimp a Butterfly*'s release during the momentous change of guard from Obama to Trump administrations and the neoconfederate turn in US politics and social life. I am interested in the ways that the schizophrenic and oppressive nature of government undergird the rapper's desire to move outside of domestic boundaries; thus, I chart the artist's expanding consciousness upon his journey to South Africa and the lessons translated to listeners about the experience. I am invested in the ways that the rapper reframes "the dark continent" as wellspring for creativity and healing, a homespace to recontextualize and reconceptualize ideas about blackness, citizenship, manhood, sanity, and freedom.

****

The cover art for *To Pimp a Butterfly* is arresting and, depending on the viewer, aspirational. Compton residents celebrate over the body of an older white judge who lays prostrate on the White House lawn with gavel in hand. The eyes of the judge are X'd out, alluding to death. The atmosphere is boisterous and high-spirited. Kendrick stands shirtless in the center of the posse, holding a small child, mouth wide open in revelry. He is nearly indistinguishable from the group of black men and boys who stand in victorious poses. They flex and boast with champagne and money stacks, some shirtless and some donning only undershirts, in front of the greatest symbol of power in the United States. The image is a literalization of the rapper's boast on "Wesley's Theory,"—*I'mma put Compton Swap Meet by The White House.* Kendrick has described the cover as taking folks who have never been outside of LA and showing them the world, a PR-friendly explanation, but there is considerably more at play.

Butterfly's cover imagines a world where a full-blown revolution has gone down. The image's grainy quality and silver-toned coloring lend an air of timelessness to the scene—at once, a defeating and defeated white supremacist past is collapsed onto a surreal projection of black (folk) future, something like a palimpsest. Possessing money, projecting joy, and occupying once-forbidden territory, Compton residents have truly risen up and made it over. Notably, the path to ascension has not required assimilation nor the shedding of street values. Boisterous and unruly blackness is the new ruling order. More explicitly, the cover suggests an anti-fascist reality where black rebellion is victorious, a striking alternative given the country's neoconfederate turn in the post-civil rights landscape. Kendrick's imagining of black power seems inherently sexist. Only with microscopic inspection does one notice the three (or so) women, faces obscured by the limbs and bodies of men, tucked into the background. This is a masculinist vision of liberation where women have been relegated to the shadows while men reap the benefits and take up the frame. *TPAB*'s artwork is subversive in its imagining of an inverted and seemingly impossible world where the intractable hierarchies of white supremacy have failed and been nullified. Here, the black underclass holds power garnered through rebellious means. Thus, the album's cover art sets the tone and theme: liberation for ghetto residents. Surely the photograph establishes the tone for the narrative that sonically unfolds by questioning who belongs in the (national) frame and what they might do when made visible within that frame.

Butterfly's cover projects an image of black power, or at least of black belonging, in the midst of an impending post-black presidency. Barack Obama was set to leave office, and Donald J. Trump was charging for the presidency, compelled by antiblack rhetoric and conspiracies like birtherism—a far right conspiracy theory that Obama was not a natural-born US citizen and, thus, was never eligible to serve as president. Trump was a career-charlatan whose desire for wealth, power, and fame would spin the country toward fascist extremes. He was a stark and demoralizing contrast to his predecessor who swept into the White House on a sea of hope and change. When Obama was elected, the future seemed so bright for those invested in liberal notions of society. We had never before seen a president like Barack Obama who was young, poised under all circumstances yet relatable. With two growing teenage daughters and the coolest wife, Obama was pretty hip for the leader of the new world. He courted hip-hop during his momentous campaign, name-dropped Kendrick as a rapper he enjoyed, and named "How Much a Dollar Cost" as his favorite track of the year. Kendrick also speaks fondly of Obama in public, saying, "Just him being in office sparks the idea that us as a people, we can do anything that we want to do. And we have smarts and the brains and the intelligence to do it."[2]

Kendrick's prominence parallels Barack Obama's presidency, and the social landscape of this momentous era is marked by a series of crises. Recovery from the Great Recession. Mass shootings in schools, churches, theaters, military bases, nightclubs, and concerts. Contaminated water and racist infrastructure. Historic patterns of hurricanes, floods, fire, and drought. Police shootings of unarmed citizens. Uprisings. At every corner Obama faced the challenge of a caricaturized self thrown back at him—the fact of his blackness was the very pinnacle of promise and the paradox of unbelonging in a country built upon antiblackness.

As a listener, I hear a profound quality of disappointment about the severe disconnect between the symbolism of

President Obama's historic achievement and the material impact of his two-term presidency for black Americans. For instance, "Institutionalized" begins with a hazy vision of the speaker who dreams himself as president of the United States.

> If I was President I'd pay my mama's rent
> Free my homies and then bulletproof my Chevy doors
> Lay in the White House and get high, Lord, Who ever thought?

The protagonist will relieve his mother of housing insecurity, release imprisoned kin, pimp out his ride, and celebrate his new capacities for power by puffing some weed—perhaps in this vision marijuana has been decriminalized and the victims of extreme drug policies remunerated. His dreams may seem shortsighted or rooted in immediate relief; however, they prove radical. Decarceration—the end of mass incarceration and abolition of prisons as a fundamental organizing principle of society—is a far more revolutionary dream than our first black president was able to achieve, let alone propose while in office.

Obama's two-term presidency did not change the ways ordinary, working-class black people were perceived and treated and prisons remained disgustingly endemic. He communed the sentences of 248 prisoners, limited the use of solitary confinement for juvenile prisoners, and visited the El Reno Federal Correctional Institute, a medium-security prison for men in Oklahoma—he was the first sitting president to visit a prison in the history of the United States. These strides for criminal justice reform were remarkably minimal in comparison to the rampaging excessiveness of the prison industrial complex. And, during his eight years in power he was unable to make any effective progress in minimizing or reforming, let alone abolishing the out-of-control prison system that undergirds our US economy. Having granted police departments even more militarized weaponry in the wake of the Ferguson Uprising, having left the issue of criminal justice reform for the last few months of his presidency, and having never satisfactorily spoken to the deep racial illness of the country after Trayvon Martin, Mike Brown Jr., and many others, some were left with lingering feelings of disappointment and confusion in the Obama-Trump transition. Given Kendrick's anti-prison ethos, when a drowsy voice cries *Massa take the chains of me!* before the bouncy beat kicks in on "Institutionalized," we must wonder if Obama is "Massa" and when the plea for freedom will be heard. The poignant lyrics of Tupac, again resurface:

> We ain't ready to have a black President
> It ain't a secret—Don't conceal the fact
> The penitentiary's packed and its filled with blacks.[3]

On the Dead Homies

Because they spirits . . . We ain't even really rapping, we just letting our dead homies tell stories for us
—*Tupac Shakur*[4]

"Hood Politics" is another standout track on Kendrick's remarkable album. As the title indicates, the rapper tackles the broad topic of politics, and as we've become accustomed to, inspects the topic with multivalent, multivoiced discernment. Each of the song's verses examines politics from a different angle—inner-city politics, state and federal politics, and finally, music industry politics. The result is a perceptive, concentrated critique of how power operates— is gained and lost, battled for, and boasted about. "Hood Politics" thinks through the ways that structural forms of violence replicate in inner-city streets. In Kendrick's estimation, gangs cannot be pinpointed as repositories of violence when law enforcement and politicians continue to prove themselves morally bankrupt and invested in blood, no matter whether "Demo-Crip" or "Re-Blood-ican." In Kendrick's experience, home is a place where emergencies are ignored ("slow motion for the ambulance"), surveillance is constant ("the project filled with cameras"), and police run an indiscriminate campaign of callousness ("LAPD gambling, scrambling, football numbers slandering"). "Hood Politics" depicts law enforcement as a corruptive force that stimulates a reckless mentality in targeted individuals.

> They give us guns and drugs, call us thugs
> Make it they promise to fuck with you
> No condom they fuck with you, Obama say, "What it do?"

At the mention of President Obama, the tempo slows to half-time and emphasizes a sludgy voice over woeful cries.

The texture and tone of this moment are striking. Kendrick's imagined utterance by Obama is paradoxical, even comical. Given that President Obama is the quintessential figure of respectability in the twenty-first century and even considered by many black people to be the dividend of integrationist strivings of the Civil Rights Movement, can you in all seriousness imagine Barack Obama saying *what it do*? On the one hand, President Obama's fictional utterance captures his complicated navigation of the black-white racial discourse that predominated his presidential tenure. On the other hand, President Obama's sobering utterance verifies his inclusion in the most elite gang set in the nation. I am reminded of Tupac's commentary during a 1995 interview recorded from Clinton Correctional:

> This country was built on gangs, you know, I think this country still is run on gangs. Republicans, Democrats, the police department, the FBI, the CIA, those are gangs, you know what I mean . . . the correctional officers. I had a correctional officer tell me straight, "We the biggest gang in New York state." Straight up.[5]

Kendrick reiterates a like-minded perspective: *From Compton to Congress, set-trippin' all around.*

For Lamar, there is a chasmic distance between the representational power of Obama's black presidency and the impact of that achievement on the lives of regular black people. I am drawn to the ways that Kendrick articulates the ambivalence of African Americans who not only witnessed Obama's inability to impart sizeable and targeted change rooted in racial justice but who also had to bear the burden of white supremacist, neoconfederate outrage. By the last years of his two-term presidency, the limitations of his power were starkly evident. The gains that he was able to accomplish felt important yet minimal in the grand scheme of things—the Ferguson Department of Justice Report on racist policing, Pell Grants for prisoners, reduced sentencing disparities between crack and powder cocaine, a $1.15 billion settlement for black farmers, about 2,000 commutations or pardons for drug convictions. President Obama's accomplishments are commendable; however, they are but a small drop in a sea of state-inflicted violence and far from the vision of true reparations for harm committed against indigenous, black, minoritized, and poor communities. The United States is in crisis as is the state of black life within the nation's border for although black people make up 13 percent of the population, black men account for 49 percent of murder victims and 41 percent of the prison population.[6] As I complete this study of *To Pimp a Butterfly* from Atlanta in the midst of a pandemic where black elders are dying and black boys stay shooting, "Hood Politics" resonates as critically urgent. Black communities are suffering and alleviation often feels beyond grasp. In the midst of this environment of deterioration, Kendrick refines the role of the artist for himself, and all of it is in memory of the dead homies.

The rapper delivers the entirety of "Hood Politics" with a shrill tone that skips sharply over the track's wavy, modulating background. For me, the rapper's high-pitched timbre and long, unrelenting lines capture the keening pitch of loss amid a distorting atmosphere.

I don't give a fuck about no politics in rap, my nigga
My little homie Stunna Deuce ain't never comin' back, my nigga
So you better go hard every time you jump on wax, my nigga

Kendrick's strong sense of purpose articulated on "Hood Politics" is animated by ongoing mourning; this kind of stark truth-telling propelled by deep hurt leaves no room for civility or passivity. This no-holds-barred approach is magnified in the closing verse, and Kendrick substantiates his position as King of the West Coast with a series of boasts that place him on par with hip-hop's legends "you askin about power, yeah, I got a lot of it / I'm the only nigga next to Snoop that can push the button." He even claims power to reanimate the infamous East Coast versus West Coast feud that resulted in the murders of two of rap's greatest, Tupac and Biggie Smalls ("I make the call, get the coast involved, then history repeats"). However, Kendrick yearns to yield power in nondestructive ways. He never pushes that button. This ideological readjustment represents a disidentificatory relationship to dominant messages within popular hip-hop, and this new mode of being and thinking is captured by an experimental musical arrangement.

The West Coast Get Down

I compare his partition-less flow as, like, a Miles Davis trumpet run—*Pharrell*[7]

At the core *To Pimp a Butterfly* is an album about expansion and much of that opening occurs at the level of sound. The musicians who elevate Kendrick's lyricism to new heights are direct descendants of LA's rich jazz legacy and call themselves the West Coast Get Down (WCGD). Notably, WCGD are of the same age group as me and Kendrick—late 1980s babies who came to age amid tough conditions in LA's black belt and who developed their musical sensibilities in relationship to the surrounding postindustrial environment. In an interview for *Dazed* digital magazine, drummer Tony Austin of the collective reflects that "Jazz was an outlet for us to express our anger. . . . Some of the other kids we knew spoke with a gun, but we used music as our language."[8] Austin and the collective express a similar relationship to place, time, and artistic expression as Kendrick, and jazz music becomes the vehicle to distill the distinctive experience of black life in Los Angeles.

The WCGD is a collective comprised of leading jazz innovators including saxophonist Kamasi Washington, producer and drummer Tony Austin, keyboardist Brandon Coleman, bassist Miles Mosley, DJ Cameron Graves, trombonist Ryan Porter, drummer Ronald Bruner Jr., and his brother Stephen Bruner (more widely known by his moniker Thundercat). When the collective entered the recording studio in 2011, they poured years of practice and improvisation into a stunning 190 track catalog in thirty short days that was distributed across eight albums, completing the debuts of Kamasi Washington (*The Epic*) and Miles Mosley (*UPRISING*), among others. Critics have marked this burst of creativity as a watershed event in jazz, one that signals fresh mainstream popularity. I was lucky enough to catch the full WCGD ensemble and associates, twenty-nine musicians including two drummers on full kits and a choir at LA's Club Nokia (renamed the Novo) in December of 2015. The experience felt like witnessing a new generation of jazz being born—it was transcendent. It is no stretch to state that these musicians of LA-based artists are repopularizing and redefining jazz for a new age of listeners and, moreover, injecting trap-heavy culture with refreshing instrumentation.

Many of the WCGD members are the children of accomplished jazz musicians who came to consciousness during the 1960s and 1970s and nurtured a revolutionary jazz spirit within their children. In interviews, Kamasi reminisces about his father allowing kids to use his garage for rehearsal—fondly calling the makeshift but generative room "The Shack." The Bruner brothers underwent intense training from their father, Ronald Bruner Sr., a drummer who played with renowned soul groups including the Supremes, the Temptations, and Gladys Knight & The Pips. LA-based community programs such as the Thelonious Monk Institute of Jazz (recently rebranded as the Herbie Hancock Institute of Jazz), a nonprofit organization founded in 1986 that is dedicated to bringing jazz to classrooms and communities around the world with programs like "Bebop to Hip-Hop" and an acclaimed International Jazz Competition, likewise nurtured members of the WCGD ensemble.

Kendrick had shown a jazz sensibility from his earliest mixtapes (see early tracks like "Compton Chemistry" or "Rigamortus"), but it wasn't until he worked with Terrace Martin for *To Pimp a Butterfly* that he began to grow confidence in the genre. The rapper remembers Martin telling him, "A lot of the chords that you picked are jazz influenced. You're a jazz musician by default. The way your cadence is rapping over certain types of snares and drums, this is everything that a person on a saxophone and a horn can meet commute with how they hear music."[9] It was Martin who brought in the WCGD collective to enhance Kendrick's vision, and as the rapper elaborates, "Stepping outside of my comfort zone and mastering it, that excited me."[10] After Kendrick had locked into a concept, he gathered the band and producers together to work from the studio for a full year, establishing a brotherhood of like-minded musicians invested in sculpting a masterpiece. Together they crafted what Kendrick estimates to be "thirty to forty songs that we fought over in the studio"[11] When Kamasi Washington was initially requested to add saxophone to "Mortal Man," he listened to the album three times in full to get a feeling and from there, changed the project's trajectory completely by weaving his influence throughout. On the band's role in the creation of *To Pimp a Butterfly*, Ronald Bruner Jr. reflects, "The way that album sounds is a love letter to all those jazz clubs we played in Crenshaw. You're hearing Kendrick rap over chords we had been honing for years. Our blood, sweat, and tears went into that record. We helped make it a masterpiece."[12] The rapper was integral to every stage of the process serving as writer, arranger, composer, and conductor. Marcus J. Moore rightly asserts, "While *To Pimp a Butterfly* was as much about the musicians as it was about Kendrick, everyone agrees that he deserves more credit as a producer."[13]

We've Been Waiting for You

This is a place that we, in urban communities, never dream of. We never dream of Africa. —*Kendrick Lamar*[14]

Kendrick Lamar traveled to South Africa in 2014 on the heels of his unprecedented success with *good kid, m.A.A.d city*, and his experiences in Johannesburg, Durban, Cape Town, and Robben Island exposed the rapper to new, clarifying knowledges. Travel "home" to the motherland solidified his belief in the musician as a mouthpiece and leader in one's community. For Kendrick, hip-hop is not only the medium for expression but the platform for transcendence from one's alienated and melancholy condition. Lamar takes listeners to where he's been—from Compton to South Africa and back again—so that his audience might better understand themselves outside of the familiar, might better recognize the few choices they've been given in their too-small worlds, and act accordingly. He finds enlightenment in South Africa and, having become versed in the country's tribal antagonisms, encounters recognition of his own gang-territorialized, institutionalized upbringing. The songs "Momma" and "How Much a Dollar Cost" most exemplify the artist's broadened sense of a diasporic self on *Butterfly*.

At one point, the working title for Kendrick's growing body of work was *How Much a Dollar Cost*, a small fact that highlights the song's importance to the narrative development of what would become *To Pimp a Butterfly*. The beat is polyrhythmic, or in other words, comprised of multiple streams of melodies that clash and cohere in exciting ways such that gaps and fissures are carved, a perfect match for Kendrick's complex flow and aptitude for rhythmic changeups. One rhythmic stream is 3/4 time, the other 4/4— the slippery, jagged nature of the track's backing beat shows sonic and thematic kinship to "Momma" such that the two resonate with one another.

The setting is a gas station in Johannesburg, and the song's conceit, or the catalyzing moment from which the narrative unfolds, is ordinary: while paying for gas, a homeless man asks Kendrick for money. The man is described as mixed-race ("semi-tan complexion") and persistent. The rapper's initial response is to write him off as a drug addict and ignore him, refusing to "Contribut[e] money just for his pipe." In this moment, Kendrick brings with him the antipathy and individualism forged in Los Angeles across the Atlantic. Instinctively, he navigates this foreign space with the mechanisms cultivated back home: a hardened exterior, distrust, and confrontation if pushed. He conflates the destitute South African and the destitute black American who suffer under different and distinct conditions. The semi-tan South African who is linked to the ruling elite by blood and language is, presumably, the victim of discriminatory post-apartheid practices that rung down on "coloured" (mixed-race) individuals. The destitute black American of Kendrick's imagination is victim to crack cocaine's devastating effects and the poverty wrought by structural racism. Though separated by distance and culture, both men are victims of racist and classist policies that uphold a caste system. In this way, Kendrick thinks through the possibility of diasporic connection despite cultural differences.

The second verse of "How Much a Dollar Cost?" pivots on the ocular (He's staring)—on being seen or unseen—and Kendrick is "feeling some kind of disrespect" at being scrutinized so closely by a stranger. Over the course of the song, the unrelenting, staring man reveals himself to be "the Messiah, the son of Jehovah," who tells Kendrick that his refusal to provide a simple dollar can cost "the price of having a spot in heaven." The rapper's morality tale asks one to consider what it truly means to navigate life in a Christlike way. He comes to conclude that a dollar can cost everything, including the soul of a man. When Kendrick queries the cost of a dollar, we would be wise to also consider the diasporic cost of (black) American wealth, or, rather, (black) American materialism that upholds corrosive colonial dynamics that diminishes black life in the United States and abroad. The dollar could cost whatever remains of the soul of this nation.

The rapper's focus on Nelson Mandela in the impending post-Obama age is striking. The listener is asked to parallel the two eloquent and charming leaders, both Nobel Peace Prize winners, whose unprecedented ascents to presidential positions captured the swelling decolonial sentiments of their respective nations. Certainly, battles for civil rights in their respective countries reflect the globalized nature of antiblack values and politics, what theorist Christina Sharpe calls *the Weather*—the climate, the totality of the atmosphere, is antiblack.[15] President Obama was voted into office in the wake of centuries of white supremacy, at once symbol of the promise of civil rights and stimulus for a neoconfederate revival. President Mandela was tasked with dismantling an apartheid minority-rule system and transitioning to a multicultural democracy, a fraught task in a country highly stratified by race and class. More important to Kendrick's narrative pulse, where Obama climbed ranks in elite institutions throughout his career as a public servant, Mandela spent twenty-seven years imprisoned, serving the majority of those years on Robben Island. When Kendrick and his crew visited Mandela's cell, I am certain that the heroic spirits of ancestors coursed through the rapper's veins, triggering an outflow of meditative material on the nature of black power, black leadership, and black love on earth. Kendrick says, "I knew I had to sit in the studio for a year or so, processing, and just create—not letting no type of boundary stop me from doing what I was doing."[16]

Jazz—in terms of instrumentation and philosophy—becomes the vehicle to express a cosmopolitan identity, one unlimited by borders of the nation-state. Certainly, with its long history of expatriatism and exchange, embedded within jazz is a destabilizing potential, one that displaces the United States as an exceptional epicenter. In her brilliant book on the very subject, Rashida Braggs deploys the term "jazz diasporas" to capture the ways in which jazz music and jazz people are inherently transnational such that fixed identities might be questioned, destabilized, and re-formed. Kendrick begins to see himself as an African American who is inextricably connected to a global community of black people—he is a citizen in and of the world (echo: *I'm African, I'm African-American*).

Butterfly draws parallels between the black American condition and that of the black South African and, in doing so, revives a discursive exchange that has faded in US popular music. Black radical musicians and their allies once wrote and performed freedom songs in support of dismantling colonial oppression at the height of Apartheid rule. These compositions brought forward issues facing Africans engaged in continental struggle to the American public, raised funds for anti-Apartheid projects, and underscored the shared realities of oppression facing black people everywhere. By the 1994 end of Apartheid rule in South Africa, vital transnational threads connecting black freedom expression across the diaspora faced withering. Kendrick revives these parched roots of black liberation expression, perhaps best heard in the song "Momma."

Lalah Hathaway's earthy backing vocals and a 3-over-4 polyrhythm creates a slippery ("sloppy") landscape within which Kendrick ripples and runs. The atmosphere is a combination of melodious, piquant, and calming. "Momma" is admittedly my favorite track on *Butterfly* because Kendrick's lyrical dexterity is on full display—he proves himself "the master that mastered it." Moreover, the narrative content of the song is divine. The song narrates from the perspective of an American speaker whose worldview shifts and expands as unfamiliar paradigms open to him. It is a track about enlightenment. The first verse attests to years of study and training, "scribbling scratching diligent sentences backwards." Thinking back to these early days, the rapper seems in awe of his development, commenting, "Now I can live in a stadium, pack it the fastest." He is filled with confidence and assures himself that "I know everything." Kendrick spends the entirety of the second verse cataloguing a comprehensive list of his wide-ranging knowledges including "wisdom," "history," "loyalty," and how "the universe work mentally." What he knows of earth, self, and spirit seems all-wise—he's knows everything—and yet, the complex rhyme patterning of the verse suggests subversion.

Kendrick rhymes *out of time* but *in the pocket*, never missing a step. By this I mean that Kendrick drops behind the melody above an already polyrhythmic beat, and the center is never lost. It's a dazzling display of virtuosity. But in the end, Kendrick embraces humility—he is no master at all. He undoes the robust mastery performed to admit, "I realized I didn't know shit / The day I came home." Travel to South Africa displaces everything within Kendrick's orbit, and when faced with a culture outside of his own, the rapper has an epiphany. He comes to understand that knowledge is a continual process of expansion, one that requires decentering of preconceived ideas and encounters with the unknown. Thus, the rapper's misaligned verse form mimic the narrative thesis: that to be *out of time*, asynchronized to the dominant way of hearing and being, *is* the method for reaching home and uncovering truth.

The *Momma* of the title is ancestral in meaning, as in the biological origin of the individual. *Momma* is also motherland—the African continent, source of blackness in the world. And for a song about language and literacy, *Momma* is also mother tongue, as in the Xulu and Xhosa tribal languages that lace *Butterfly*; as in the black vernacular of Compton, California made popular through gangster rap. The polysemous nature of *Momma* disrupts the idea of a stable, identifiable location for the protagonist and suggests the possibility for a multiplicity of home spaces for the alienated black artist.

The Grammy Awards, Redux

The West is not the West. It is a project, not a place.
—*Édouard Glissant*[17]

In early 2016, confident about the milestone achievements of *Butterfly*, Kendrick expressed desire to insert himself into history, saying, "When we think about the Grammys, only Lauryn Hill and OutKast have won Album of the Year. This would be big for hip-hop culture at large."[18] He was nominated for eleven awards, the most any rapper had ever achieved in a single night, and was aiming to "win them all." While he didn't join Ms. Hill and OutKast, losing Album of the Year to Taylor Swift's *1989*, he did insert himself into history by performing a militant message on a conservative stage where he had previously experienced a form of racial violence (re: the Macklemore debacle).

> I approach my stage performance the same way I approach the studio—I have to think about it and live it and know how my mannerisms are, you know, how I'm moving.

All that has to be dead on to me, from the hits and the licks to how we rearrange the music to give the fans a new experience, it's a process. The same way I sit with mixes and mastering, that's the same way I sit inside the rehearsal room to make sure that everything is hitting on cue.[19]

Undeniably, the most powerful public performance that Kendrick gave in promotion for *To Pimp a Butterfly* was for the 58th Annual Grammy Awards in the spring of 2016. Imagine: The rapper shuffles from upstage in a prison-blue jumpsuit, chained at the ankles and wrists to a coffle of men who shuffle in step behind. Two spotlights reveal the setting as a prison. On either side of the chain gang, men in prison blues look out from the bars of their cells. Everyone is black. The sound of scuffling chains and the wail of a sorrowful saxophone punctuate the haunting scene. When the rapper finally reaches the microphone at down center, Kendrick painstakingly heaves the heavy chains that bind his wrists up and around the microphone to better perform. The task is laborious, the room is silent, and, in this moment, Kendrick has the world's attention.

Suddenly he launches into an a cappella delivery of the first verse of "The Blacker the Berry," taking his time to breathe through and clearly articulate every searing word. The artist's performance is sincere and unflinching. Even with well-placed revisions that tame the most vulgar language of the song, the message is clear: *You sabotage my community & make a killing / You made me a killer, emancipation of real hitta.* At this moment Kendrick and his enchained companions break loose of their heavy chains. Black light reveals neo-tribal markings that obscure the prison blues. The men glow like Maasai warriors in the midst of ritual— they dance in powerful displays of control and agility, bone-breaking limbs in defiance of linear movement.

As if in a dream state, the sound of African drums lulls the rapper through a woozy transition. Encircled by women in tribal costumes who perform traditional West African dance steps, Kendrick moves into his anthem "Alright," performing both exhilarating verses of the song. Dianne Garcia, Kendrick's stylist, has discussed the symbolism of the African costumery, saying:

> [T]he girls, the dancers, they have red paint painted all over their body and that's inspired specifically by the Himba tribe in Northern Namibia. They wear this red paint that's supposed to represent the color of the earth and the blood. And we picked the Himba tribe basically because [they are] really strong women who do all the labor work while taking care of their own homes and all this stuff while the men are out herding cattle and doing politics.[20]

The rapper heavily censors the song's memorable pre-chorus, taking all mention of "niggas," "guns," and "po-po's" out such that much of the militant lyrical content that embraces any possibility of armed rebellion is evacuated. But Kendrick brings it back to a central message of liberation with his final transition and closing a cappella poem. After the fiery and energetic quality of "Alright," the rapper moves to center stage to deliver a previously unheard verse of an untitled song beneath a beaming spotlight. The camera focuses on the rapper in a tight shot, and the audience sees for the first time that Kendrick's eye is blackened. He says, "On February 26th I lost my life too"—a line that hurtles the audience back to four years prior when seventeen-year-old Trayvon Martin was stalked and gunned down by George Zimmerman, a white-Hispanic vigilante surveilling his Sanford, Florida neighborhood. He notes, "This is modern day slavery." The verse unfolds as a revenge plot: the rapper has set his sights on Zimmerman (presumably) and he watches him through the window, plotting next steps. "You leave your briefcase on the couch, that's why I plan on creeping through your damn door / And blowing out every damn piece of your brain." In Kendrick's narrative, when a small child runs into the window frame, he abandons his gory plot for vengeance. In this previously unreleased verse, the rapper pours out a mixture of pent-up hurt and fury, indicting the viewing audience in the process: "You wanna see a good man with a broken heart." The last line of Kendrick's verse and the performance—"Conversation for the entire nation. This is bigger than us"—is as impactful as the closing image that emblazes Kendrick's silhouetted figure (Figure 1).

Body bold in silhouette, Kendrick stands in front of the black-and-white image of Africa that glows like a moon in a starless sky. The single word "Compton" is typed in calligraphic letters across the expanse of the continent's northern hemisphere, and the words of the rapper's opening reverberate—*I'm African American, I'm African / I'm black as the moon, heritage of small village.* There is no marker on the continent that ties Compton to a specified location—All of Africa *is* Compton or Compton

Figure 3.1 Kendrick Lamar at the 58th Annual Grammy Awards by Kevin Winter © Getty Images.

is all of Africa. The image is aspirational, empowering, and, like the medley of singles performed on this night, deeply ambiguous. A call for Pan-African consciousness; A call for repatriation; A denouncement of America as home that has never been home . . . All of these possibilities exude from the powerful closing image.

Kendrick's stunning Grammy performance was widely applauded as historic and impactful; however, the performance was also met with critique from some voices because of the Africa-Compton image. These critiques are legitimate and stimulated good discourse among black folk in venues like Twitter. The image erases borders of countries, presenting what might be called a utopian vision of a united nation and consequently erases the diversity of Africa—its cultures, languages, ethnic groups, geopolitics, etc. Resultingly, the textured particularity that exists among Africans is collapsed into an undifferentiated mass. Sculpted for an American audience, this image could serve to reinforce the ignorance of Africa that exists in the United States where there is a discernable and disconcerting absence of colonial discourse. Too often, African Americans are taught to see themselves as distinctive and distinguished. We are taught to harbor internalized stigmas and to be in competition over scant resources—we adopt the value systems of our oppressors and, in doing so, think ourselves exceptional, superior. Africa is reinforced as a source of disease, savagery, underdevelopment, and hunger in the mind of the (black) American and Pan-African formations have trouble taking root, blossoming, and flourishing.

Arguably, the Africa-Compton message is uneven and romantic; however, it is nonetheless *sincere*. Kendrick says,

> I felt like I belonged in Africa. I saw all the things that I wasn't taught. Probably one of the hardest things to do is put [together] a concept on how beautiful a place can be and tell a person this while they're still in the ghettos of Compton. I wanted to put that experience in the music.[21]

I want to leave room for a paradigm that allows serious engagement with the sincerity of Kendrick's conceptual album and his strivings to widen the horizons of *institutionalized* individuals. When contextualized within the artist's larger anti-capitalist and decarceral pursuit, Kendrick's Pan-African celebration on the Grammy stage takes on a disruptive quality that destabilizes power and reorients the homespace for black Americans. The rapper's diasporic embrace, his willingness to exchange knowledge, brush against, and think through his relationship to ancestral land describes what political scientist Richard Iton calls *diasporic conviviality*.[22] I am interested in the extent to which this element of sincere diasporic conviviality might threaten a normative social order by disordering and recontextualizing the signs and symbols of the nation, itself a project of modernity.

Following the great anthropologist and historian Michel-Rolph Trouillot (who himself is following renowned theorist Édouard Glissant), if we understand the West not as a *place* but as a *project*, then we may also understand how this project relies upon the notion of the Other. Trouillot distinguishes *geographies of management*, the creation of bounded and definable places such as nations, territories, and cities, from *geographies of imagination*, the perpetuation of a particular image of modernity, an imaginary West. Thus, the United States as an idea projected to the world is distinguished from the nation itself a geographical entity. In this project of the West, there exists no Western ideal without the "Other," and in the United States, there is no more quintessential an Other than "the nigger." In Trouillot's words, "[Modernity] requires another from within, the otherwise modern."[23]

Kendrick's closing statement on the Grammy stage brings awareness to how sites like Compton and the African continent, together, are othered as a corrupt and corrupting project of the West, one that makes niggers of men and women. In other words, he underscores how the nation-state as a project of Western modernity is intrinsically antiblack. In linking "the nigger" to the *institutionalized* and to the *pimped*, Kendrick highlights how racial capitalism requires an expendable "surplus" population that is mined for resources and profit before ultimate disposal. And for Lamar, liberation from this maddening condition must be forged beyond the nation as we currently understand it, a project of reconceptualization that involves seismic shifts in how America sees itself in relationship to the (black) world.

Of that night and the rapper's brilliant performance, director Ava DuVernay (who also hails from the black homespace of Compton, California) tweeted:

Kendrick was electric. But didn't get the love deserved inside Staples. Was kinda quiet in here. My sis + I went wild tho. #Compton #GRAMMYs[24]

The rapper's performance provoked deep feeling and certainly unease in the viewing audience filled with elite Academy members. It was a message that asked viewers to move beyond the tepid racial conversation of the present into a more radical process of self-recognition, accountability, destabilization, and transnational alliance-building. What other Billboard-charting rapper can you point to who so provocatively thinks through the possibilities for Pan-African solidarities; about the precarity of the black artists within a global market; about the ways that racial capitalism is an extended colonial project? In the American popular music landscape, Kendrick is exemplary, a shining moon lighting the sky.

Internalized Racism

Tupac's "Keep Ya Head Up" is one of the most enduring uplift songs of rap's fifty-year span, and Kendrick clearly had the song on his mind when he titled a track on *Butterfly* after Pac's memorable first lines "Some say the blacker the berry, the sweeter the juice / I say the darker the flesh, the deeper the roots."[25] "Keep Ya Head Up" celebrates the beauty and resilience of black people who "ain't meant to survive 'cause it's a set up"—Tupac speaks directly to the downtrodden, "sisters on welfare" and the black men who mistreat female counterparts. Where he calls upon women to continue their support of black men despite under-recognition and abuse, he also calls for men to reevaluate dominant actions, saying that "real men" work to "heal our women." Rapsody also had

"Keep Ya Head Up" on her mind when she penned her verse to *Butterfly*'s "Complexion (A Zulu Love)." Together Kendrick and Rapsody extend the legacy of Tupac's uplift mission by confronting barriers to black heterosexual love, calling for transformation in the ways companions relate to one another.

"Complexion" continues a narrative of enlightenment gained from experiences in South Africa where Kendrick's exposure to an alternative history of discrimination based on skin color and tribal affiliation prompts deep consideration of solidarity among black Americans in the United States. The track highlights the colonial origins of "colorism"—a term coined by Pulitzer Prize winner Alice Walker who again shows influence in Kendrick's world. Colorism is a manifestation of internalized racism where communities minoritized under colonial regimes come to evaluate their own according to white standards. In colorist formations, phenotypic traits such as dark skin tone, wide noses, and kinky hair are devalued in preference for European features. The prevalence of skin lightening creams throughout Asia and Africa is but one example of how colorism appears in the lives of people of color. Compulsive respectability, skewed body image, and poor self-esteem are some of the damaging results of colorism and internalized racism. From the quality of medical care to prison sentencing, income prospects and romantic options, colorism continues to impact the lives and outcomes of black men and women in profound ways.

"Complexion" adds nuance to an album invested in examining white supremacy by suggesting that movement toward liberation requires the eradication of racism's lingering byproducts within oneself. Kendrick shows investment in unpacking the relationship between controlling social structures and the ordinary people who live under those oppressive operations. The rapper declares, "Give a fuck about your complexion, I know what the Germans done" such that connection of the United States, South Africa, and Nazi Germany condemns countries guilty of instituting racial and ethnic castes and committing heinous acts upon targeted groups.

Surprisingly, "Complexion" is the only track that features a full guest verse on the record, an eye-opening fact when one considers the collaborative impulse of the album. Kendrick's choice for co-conspirator is deliberate; he remembers, "Immediately when I heard the beat I heard [Rapsody's] voice and vocal tone. But what made her special was that I knew that she was going to bring the content from a woman's perspective about complexion, being insecure and at the same time having gratitude for your complexion."[26] Rapsody has her own memories of the track's making. She remarks, "[Kendrick] wanted to talk about the beauty of black people. I told him to say no more. What tripped me out is Kendrick originally said that he didn't want to do a verse on there. He wanted me to do two verses and Prince to do the hook."[27] I find this backstory of mutual recognition and respect so telling of Kendrick's character, compositional process, and intention. Rapsody is a thoughtful and skilled lyricist who brings a refreshing dimensionality to a rap industry that rewards sex-oriented performances by women. Signed to Roc Nation, she is, perhaps, the solitary prominent female rapper whose philosophy and ethical commitment align with Kendrick's, an observation that does not cast judgment upon black women's performances but, rather, illuminates the patriarchal nature of the music industry.

"Complexion" is a kind of love song composed of gorgeous imagery and poetic lines that magnify the exquisiteness of black skin tones—*Dark as the midnight hour or bright as the morning sun*. The setting is a plantation and the song opens in the voice of an antebellum slave who is courting a woman. The listener finds themselves in a world where a racial caste system is sharply delineated and consequences for crossing the color line can be deadly. Within this matrix of dehumanization and threat, Kendrick's persona is full of cunning, vigor, and desire:

Sneak me through the back window, I'm a good field nigga
I made a flower for you out of cotton just to chill with you

His love interest is mixed-race, presumed to be the product of an enslaved woman and a lecherous master ("Brown skinned but your blue eyes telling me your mama can't run"). Like Morrison's Sixo of Sweet Home,[28] the protagonist commits to dangerous action in the name of black love. He brings small gifts of affection to his lover and vows to risk life and limb for her "even if master listening." He insists, "I'm a good field nigga," showing his willingness to cross boundaries and outwardly perform passivity in the name of love. I adore how "Complexion" reminds listeners of radical forms of love that persisted amid cruel, inhumane conditions, and I am taken with the rapper's illumination of love forged within a freedom-seeking context.

I view Kendrick and Rapsody's exchange on "Complexion" as one form of a healthy dialogue between black men and black women about healing wounds that recycle in our lives and relationships. When Kendrick raps that "I'ma say something that's vital and critical for survival / of mankind." he underscores how the damage of colonialism lies not only the (re)production of racism but in the upholding of patriarchy. In this song, tenderness, compassion, and devotion are valued characteristics that honor ancestral wisdom and heal generational trauma. Scholar bell hooks writes, "one of the primary achievements of [the] black power movement was the critique and, in some instances, dismantling color-caste hierarchies."[29] Rapsody and Kendrick extend the "black is beautiful" ethos of the black power generation in their honoring of the manifold hues, shades, and tones of blackness. To embrace love as a method for liberation is, perhaps, the most subversive gift a rap artist could give to his audience when bravado—economic and sexual—is the most valued and authenticating quality of the rap genre. Kendrick's conception of love is one that extends from self-knowledge, and this coming-to-consciousness involves reckoning in regard to embedded beliefs and destructive values.

I Love Myself

The freedom to want your own particular hip self is
a freedom of a somewhat different and more difficult
nature.—*Amiri Baraka*[30]

Although it is the last song I address on the album and the track that closes *Butterfly*'s narrative, "i" dropped as the first single a full six months ahead of *To Pimp a Butterfly*'s official March 2015 release. The lead single garnered two Grammy awards for "Best Rap Performance" and "Best Rap Song," and still, the album hadn't yet dropped. The anticipation to see what Kendrick was coming with for his sophomore follow-up was thick and weighty. For some fans who relished the grit and 808-heavy nature of *good kid*, they wondered about the buoyant Isley's sample and divergent aesthetic "i" seemed to embrace. Was Kendrick going in a new direction? Was he going pop? On the tails of his crossover guest appearance on Taylor Swift's "Bad Blood," some were quick to be critical. In response to the skeptics, Kendrick has simply offered, "I grow. I'm like a chameleon. That is a gift and a curse for me."[31]

The cover art for the single is simple and arrestingly beautiful. Two black men are pictured from the waist down wearing oppositional colors, the crisp red and blue bandanas from their pockets signify oppositional gang affiliation. These men throw up new kinds of signs by shaping their fingers into hearts. The picture's close-cropped framing reveals that this is a portrait, and rather than center the face, viewers are called to consider the hands. The image illustrates Kendrick's determination to heal divisions in Compton and instill messages of beauty and pride in listeners, to "spark the idea of some kind of change through music or through me," the rapper reflects.[32] For Kendrick, the fierce love of one's black self is threatening to a power structure heavily invested in perpetuating myths about itself and its great society.

Furthermore, his message of liberating love has the power to save lives in a society plagued by mental illness and violence.

Self-described as "raised off the Isley's,"[33] Kendrick is a "post soul-baby"[34] who shines with pride when addressing the musical choices made for "i" like his idea to sample "That Lady" and then fly to St. Louis to gain copyright permission in person, and more importantly, a blessing from balladeer Ronald Isley. Perhaps most important to Kendrick's project of reimaging soul is his decision to incorporate live instrumentation that interpolates, rather than loops the sample. The band's reinterpretation provides depth and shading and yields room for improvisation within a well-known feel-good classic, a point to which I will shortly return.

"i" is a song about triumph, self-confidence, hope, and redemption. In the narrative cycle, the protagonist has defeated his foes and celebrates his own hip self. He "Blows steam in the face of the beast" and boastfully asserts, "Look at me, motherfucker, I smile." When I hear Kendrick so unabashedly claim his smile, my world opens and even I, a self-proclaimed sullen girl with a pessimistic worldview, can believe in a loving world. Hip-hop culture has come a long way from the atmosphere that caused Tupac to reflect, "I'm just a nigga on his own / Living life thugstyle, so I can't smile."[35] For Tupac and others of his generation, to live *thugstyle* with a hardened, impenetrable exterior was a necessary defense for a brutal reality. As heir apparent, Kendrick understands that it is a necessary tool of survival to be in touch with one's interiority, to embrace difficult feelings, and to move beyond the veneer of masculine hardness. *Realness* is in fact raw, but it is also multifaceted and deep feeling and deep thinking. Realness is vulnerable.

The music video that accompanies "i" is simple, textured, and sublime. The scene is late at night in a darkly lit neighborhood bar. Folks are doing what folks do after hours; they dance and flirt and commune. Kendrick sits in the midst of it all as a woman braids his hair into cornrows. He is quiet and observant. Suddenly a fight breaks out between two men, one wearing blue, the other red. This moment of contention is catalyst—the up-tempo, guitar-driven melody of the Isley's "That Lady" kicks in and Kendrick rises to dance.

Kendrick performs what should be regarded as a signature dance—he blends a recognizable Crip-Walk, a dance born from gang sets that focuses on angular footwork, with Chicago Stepping, a smooth and fluid partner dance that derives from swing and bop styles. In some camps Kendrick was clowned for his seemingly untraditional, old-school dance moves; however, most critics missed the point entirely. The rapper's signature dance is a remixed composition that encompasses the roots of who he is—LA and gang-affiliated by way of Chicago; black and assured; a nimble-bodied product of the old school who is ready to lead an army via love. The rapper catches a groove so hypnotic that he glides away from the bar and out into the streets where bystanders find themselves likewise caught in the groove. The mass of dancers swells as they move through the streets, and this midnight display of jubilance counteracts any darkness encountered. The dancers disrupt a police arrest in progress; a scene of domestic violence; a distraught man holding a gun to his own temple. These somber scenes that unfold in the dark cover of night are upturned through the kinesthetic pleasure of dance and empowering presence of community. The song's anti-suicide message and celebration of black aliveness are direct and sincere, and, yet, like all of Kendrick's work, elements of darkness pervade all levels of the song: instrumentation, lyrics, and visuals.

When Ronald Isley[36] makes a cameo in the video, replete in his Mr. Bigg's pimp iconography, he takes the rapper for a ride in his blood-red Cadillac that gleams in the dark and empty streets. Kendrick hangs his upper body out of the Caddy's backseat window, his shirt a stark white in this midnight hour, and he is feverish; he sweats and spits; his arms flail and head lolls—at times his eyes roll to the back of his head. Kendrick oscillates between controlled rage and unconscious relief and his manic, unpredictable performance is disquieting. This moment feels dangerously loaded with explosive energy. The love of oneself threatens to induce a delirium so potent that there may be no return.

N.E.G.U.S.

I want to explain to people that when they do get over the wall, *leave*, but come back and pick up your friends.[37]—
Ice-T, 1994

There are, in fact, two versions of "i." When the album dropped six months after the single, the song had been altered to create a dynamic imitation of a live performance. Kendrick closes the narrative arc with a community concert, one that embodies the ideals of peace and brotherhood that he's strived toward over the course of *To Pimp a Butterfly*. Like its counterpart "u," the track is theatrical such that a story is staged and dramatized, packaged for the audience to meditate upon the very nature of its construction. The differences between the two versions are strategic and effective. Kendrick performs with energetic, full volume vocals, and the backing singers take the refrain to extraordinary heights—*I love myself!* they belt in funky harmony. A hype man opens the song welcoming "nobody . . . nobody . . . nobody but the number one rapper in the world!" Over the hum of a crowd, the hype man builds anticipation saying, "He done traveled all over the world / He came back just to give you some game." The hype man calls all the boys and stage to the front of the stage to receive the message of self-love that will unfold. This welcome builds a palpable connection between the audience and rapper, collapsing distance between celebrity and neighborhood kid, celebrity and listener. Kendrick has returned home, and he has messages of redemption for his people, for all of us.

Counterbalanced against "u," this live interpolation emphasizes that "i" is inherently connected to "we," and it is an *i* of relationality. For Kendrick, "i" is a self-referential performance that celebrates music's capacity to bring listeners back from brink of breaking, which makes one reconsider their inherent value and place in the world. "i" actualizes Kendrick's role as a leader for his community, one whose destiny is connected to others beyond the egocentric self. I am taken with the lowercase presentation of "i" and "u" that simultaneously hearkens back to artists like 2Pac and Prince who stylized their writing by typographically blackening the English language. Simultaneously, "i" and "u" minimize the ego. Distinguished from "I," Kendrick's lowercase lettering signifies humility in the midst of self-actualization where "i' reflects a coming to *one's own hip self* such that egocentricity is displaced in lieu of community. This is Kendrick's liberationist love ethic—knowing and adoring the self; extending the self outward in love and compassion; reveling in the exquisite nature of unruly, unbounded blackness. This love is unabashed, joyful, rageful, aspirational, and unveiled—it's all of that.

One of the more considerable departures is the song's chorus which keeps the refrain but morphs in lyrical content entirely, especially with the line "I put a bullet in the back of the head of the *police*" (alternatively interpreted as "back of the head of the *bully*"). The rapper squawks and screeches, letting the guttural sounds of the ecstatic flow. When he reworks the chorus to urge, "Illuminated by the hand of God, boy don't be shy," I hear the artist assure himself and listeners that submission to spirit is a transformative endeavor. I am thinking about how the very act of remaking a single that has already been canonized by listening audience into a new, fresh object of discernment is an act that expresses allegiance to one's principled, divine purpose. Self-reflection coupled with recalibration is godly work.

The closing skit embedded within the live album version of "i" provides some of the richest material for digestion on the album. The dramatic climax of the song occurs when the third verse, delivered at a breakneck pace, is cut short because a fight has erupted in the crowd. The music cuts out and

Kendrick quickly gains control of the situation by delivering a compelling "a cappella" verse, what I call a performance poem. Kendrick moves the crowd to quietude by asking, "How many niggas we done lost? This year alone? Exactly. See we ain't got time to waste my nigga." He centers on the condition of mourning as one that links listeners together in a kinship of loss. I find this meaningful given how grief catalyzes feelings of isolation and alienation, even if mortality is the human condition that underlies all of our experiences. He is frank and fearless in his address: "All this to say because I love you niggas, man. I love all my niggas, bro."

I am interested in the ways that the culminating per-formance poem interrogates language as a tool of communi-cation and power, a tool that can be reframed and reformed. The rapper utilizes the space of the skit to defamiliarize the word "nigger," a term that through hip-hop culture has become ubiquitous such that linguistic policing of its boundaries in this day and age seems futile. For Kendrick, language has been weaponized as a colonial tool ("America tried to make it to a house divided / The homies don't recognize we been using it wrong"). and education in the United States has been incomplete and inaccurate ("The history books overlook the word and hide it"), ultimately eliding the predominance of antiblackness. i" and its skit suggest that healing fractured communities begins with recovery of a true and noble self that is untainted by colonial disinformation. Listeners are reminded of the prominence of the N-word throughout *Butterfly*, from the opening sample, *every nigger is a star*, to America's berating verbal attack, *nigga, you ain't shit*. By the end of *Butterfly*'s narrative, Kendrick incorporates new knowledge gained from diasporic exposure, modeling how deep study can contribute positively to one's life. Like Richard Pryor and Dave Chappelle before him, Kendrick Lamar proposes to abandon the word, having come to an awakening about how language divides and distracts from the project of brotherhood. Again, I turn to Tupac Shakur who retooled the word "nigga" to mean "Never Ignorant, Getting Goals Accomplished" on his jazz-infused track "Words of Wisdom" from his debut *2Pacalypse Now*. Lamar also draws a spotlight on the term and, instead, introduces the alternative "Negus," going on to spell it for the crowd and provide a breakdown of the word's Ethiopian origin and meaning: "royalty . . . black emperor, king, ruler." With this meditation I am reminded that Kendrick is the living, breathing possibility of what Tupac could have grown into. He had so much potential. Imagine if more than the ashes of Tupac traveled to South Africa. Imagine if Tupac were able to meet Nelson Mandela (as his mother Afeni did), or Barack Obama, for that matter. Imagine if martyrdom didn't require flesh. Imagine. This is what Kendrick Lamar's work compels listeners to do: imagine.

Afterword

I've illuminated the blackness of my invisibility—
and vice versa.
—*Ralph Ellison*[1]

As a professor of English at Spelman College, a leading HBCU (Historical Black College and University), I would be remiss if I didn't end on a literary note. *To Pimp a Butterfly* is certainly a "literary" album in that Lamar not only continues building upon the autobiographical coming of age story laid out on *good kid, m.A.A.d city*, but he also weaves a syllabus of African American intellectualism into his bildungsroman of consciousness and growth.

For instance, "i" and "The Blacker the Berry" can be viewed as an embodiment of *double consciousness*, a foundational theory of Black Studies coined by premier sociologist W. E. B. Du Bois. Double consciousness describes the state of living-while-black in a country that misrecognizes black people—it captures the experience of being representationally sculpted and thus socially constrained; the "sense of always looking at one's self through the eyes of others."[2] For Du Bois, a doubled subjectivity is both a curse and a blessing for, on the one hand, negotiating how one sees the black subject is mentally, spiritually, and physically exhausting. On the other hand, double consciousness endows the black subject with "second sight"—the tools and vision for navigating and, thus, resisting racial oppression. Kendrick examines how subjectivity is nourished from within and can be undone from without, how blackness is a condition inducing both pride and rage. Focusing on the deep depression from which he has suffered and the methods for moving toward deliverance, *To Pimp a Butterfly* visits both sides of the veil and embraces this second sight as a source of power.

I like to imagine that Kendrick is an avid reader, although he admits to preferring dialogue with living people over written text. However, it is evident that particular books of the African American tradition have contributed to shaping Kendrick as an entertainer and individual. He recalls the effects that Alex Hayley's *The Autobiography of Malcolm X* had on his artistry as a teenager, saying, "That was the first idea that inspired how I was going to approach my music. From the simple idea of wanting to better myself by being in this mind-state, [the] same way Malcolm was."[3] Harper Lee, Alex Hayley, Wallace Thurman, Alice Walker, and Tupac himself are all literary allusions embedded within *Butterfly*'s muscular body.

Perhaps Kendrick was reading *Invisible Man* on tour, or perhaps it's a novel that has stuck with him over time—it is the kind of book that will do that, beg you to come back to it with every new life stage one enters. In my class "Seminal Writers of the African American Tradition," I teach *Invisible Man*, all 500+ pages of it, twice a year and it's a book that changed the direction of my life, thus, I was excited when "King Kunta" cites *Invisible Man* in a nuanced, powerful way (*what's the yams?!*). The story of *Invisible Man* is one that remains relevant: a young black man attempts to find his place in society but, at every turn, finds racism limiting his possibilities and distorting his vision—in the historically black university, the blue-collar workforce, leftist political organizations—no matter the realm in which he enters, destructive ideologies humiliate and alienate the protagonist. He undergoes a series of rites that bring him closer to the realization that he must act out of his own convictions or else, remain a powerless pawn to be manipulated from without— "simply a material, a natural resource to be used."[4] He concludes that he alone is responsible for his self-definition and, furthermore, is capable of moving strategically in the fugitive spaces of society (underground). Synchronicities between Ellison and Kendrick's protagonists reveal an ongoing and unfolding mode of black aesthetic discourse in the United States. Both long-form works narrate the coming-to-consciousness, replete with humiliations and victories, of a nameless protagonist who, in some ways, is representative of the artist themselves, and, in both works, this coming-to-consciousness is presented in spiraling, experimental jazz form.

Kendrick's inclusion of Ellison is poignant and underscores the ways that black men in the United States experience a paradoxical state of invisibility and hypervisibility, at once relegated to liminal, subservient positions in the economic sector while lauded for extraordinary performances in entertainment fields such as sports and music. Furthermore, in our technological age, all citizens of the United States live with the condition of increased visibility—everyone has a handheld camera built into their phones and surveillance fuses with ordinary life. The sense that one is always being watched and that one may be the watcher at any moment is pervasive. Coupled with the quotidian quality of social media networking, society has become increasingly performative. More disturbingly, surveillance technology is the vehicle for increased visibility of deadly encounters between unarmed black citizens and law enforcement officers. Altogether, processes of sight are central to how black men are rendered and, thus, dictate movement.

Ellison has discussed how his seminal novel was, in part, inspired by seeing advertisement for a "Tom show," a minstrel performance which he assumed would, by the 1940s, be a thing of the past. Perhaps feeling the mixture of "dormant, dusted, doomed, disgusted" that Kendrick testifies to in "For Free?," *Invisible Man* is the brilliantly mordant exposition that followed. Ellison's interest in controlling images like the Sambo figure asks readers to consider the ways that stereotypes are fashioned and refashioned in response to the social landscape and its demands of the time. When Kendrick's figure is superimposed with the Sambo (see "For Free?"), he pulls forth Ellison's observations on the enduring nature of controlling derogatory images, especially for the black performer.

In his autobiographical compositional impulses, Kendrick extends what Kathy Lou Shultz calls the tradition of the "Afro-modernist Epic" as animated in the experimental works of figures like Langston Hughes, Amiri Baraka, and Melvin B. Tolson.[5] Marvelously, he has written himself into musical and literary canons populated by heroes. Ellison and Lamar share special honors for their timely, impactful writing. *Invisible Man* is the first book by an African American writer to win the National Book Award, and, seventy years following, Kendrick Lamar is the first rap artist to win the Pulitzer Prize. In 2017, *To Pimp a Butterfly* was selected by 9th Wonder to be archived at Harvard's W. E. B. Du Bois Institute along with three other classic albums: A Tribe Called Quest's *The Low End Theory*, Nas's *Illmatic* (1994), and Lauryn Hill's *The Miseducation of Lauryn Hill* (1998).

As I finish this book having lived and protested through the Obama-Trump years, and as I prepare for the decades of aftermath before me, I am grateful that *To Pimp a Butterfly* persists as an acclaimed artifact of genius. As an LA girl and longtime lyricist-lover, I'm pleased to boast Kendrick as one of the best living rappers and one of the most special to have ever entered the industry. He is a genius and I'm proud to celebrate that talent while living in a nation that makes martyrs of courageous, kin-loving black men. The comparison of Kendrick to rappers to Top-5 rappers like Nas, Rakim, and Jay-Z is more than appropriate, and it is not too early to deem *To Pimp a Butterfly* a masterwork and defining artifact of the unfolding twenty-first century. My hope is that Kendrick Lamar has inspired a generation of rap listeners like myself to read more, travel farther, self-examine, and strive toward individual and collective greatness in all endeavors.

Notes

Dedication

1   Tricia Rose, *Black Noise: Rap Music and Black Culture in Contemporary America*, Illustrated ed. (Hanover, NH: Wesleyan University Press, 1994), 185.

Preface

1   The biogenesis of this project is my dissertation project, *Liberation Aesthetics in the #BlackLivesMatter Era: Poetry, Protest and Social Justice*, a title I provide in full because what compelled my early, messy attempts to capture the exquisiteness of Kendrick's artistry has never tempered: Liberation. Freedom. Self-definition. Sovereignty.

2   Breakfast Club Power 105.1 FM, *Kendrick Lamar Talks Overcoming Depression, Responsibility to the Culture* (New York, 2015), https://www.youtube.com/watch?v=nVtH55HizPM.

Chapter 1

1   James Baldwin and Studs Terkel. "An Interview with James Baldwin," in *James Baldwin: The Last Interview and Other Conversations* (Brooklyn; London: Melville House, 2014).

2   Recording Academy, *Kendrick Lamar Nomination Interview | 58th GRAMMYs*, 2016, https://www.youtube.com/watch?v=oB747PvKae0.

3   GQ, *Kendrick Lamar Meets Rick Rubin and They Have an Epic Conversation* (Malibu, CA: Shangri-La Studio, 2016), https://www.youtube.com/watch?v=4lPD5PtqMiE.

4   Ibid.

5   Andreas Hale, "The Oral History of Kendrick Lamar's 'To Pimp a Butterfly,'" *Cuepoint at Medium*, September 8, 2016, https://medium.com/cuepoint/the-oral-history-of-kendrick-lamar-s-to-pimp-a-butterfly-622f725c3fde.

6   XXL, "Writer at War: Kendrick Lamar's XXL Cover Story," *XXL Magazine*, January 6, 2015, https://www.xxlmag.com/writer-war-kendrick-lamar-own-words/.

7   For an interesting history on the making, distribution, and disappearance of the 1974 film *Every Nigger Is a Star* and its accompanying album, see Erica Moiah James, "Every Nigger Is a Star: Reimagining Blackness from Post-civil Rights America to the Postindependence Caribbean," *Black Camera* 8, no. 1 (2016): 55–83.

8   Mark Anthony Neal, *What the Music Said: Black Popular Music and Black Public Culture* (New York: Routledge, 1998), 21.

9   Dominique Leone, "Funkadelic: Funkadelic / Free Your Mind / Maggot Brain / America Eats Its Young," *Pitchfork*, August 3, 2005,

https://pitchfork.com/reviews/albums/11739-funkadelic-free-your
-mind-maggot-brain-america-eats-its-young/.

10   Francesca T. Royster, "Here's a Chance to Dance Our Way
     Out of Our Constrictions: P-Funk's Black Masculinity and
     the Performance of Imaginative Freedom," *Poroi, Sexing the
     Colorlines: Black Sexualities, Popular Culture, and Cultural
     Production* 7, no. 2 (June 2011): 23.

11   Borrowed phrasing from Imani Perry, *Prophets of the Hood:
     Politics and Poetics in Hip Hop* (Durham: Duke University
     Press, 2004).

12   Breakfast Club Power 105.1 FM, *Kendrick Lamar Talks
     Overcoming Depression, Responsibility to the Culture* (YouTube).

13   Ice-T, "The Jungle Creed," *The Ice Opinion: Ice T*, ed. Heidi
     Siegmund (New York: St Martin's Press, 1994), 21.

14   Slick Rick, *The Great Adventures of Slick Rick* (New York: Def
     Jam Recordings, 1988).

15   Hale, "The Oral History of Kendrick Lamar's 'To Pimp a
     Butterfly.'"

16   See Tupac Shakur's poem, "Loving Is Just Complicated," in
     The Rose That Grew from Concrete (New York: Pocket Books,
     1999), 63–4.

17   Songs like DMX's "Slippin'," Geto Boys's "Mind Playing Tricks
     on Me," Biggie's "Suicidal Thoughts," Lil Wayne's "I Think of
     Dying," and A Tribe Called Quest's "Stressed Out" are a few
     standout tracks that address mental health in hip-hop.

18   XXL, "Writer at War: Kendrick Lamar's XXL Cover Story."

19   Public Enemy, *Fear of a Black Planet* (New York: Def Jam
     Recordings, 1990).

20   Perry A. Hall, "African-American Music: Dynamics of
     Appropriation and Innovation," in *Borrowed Power: Essays on*

Cultural Appropriation, ed. Bruce H. Ziff and Pratima V. Rao (New Brunswick, NJ: Rutgers University Press, 1997), 31–51.

21 Ibid., 32.

22 Hale, "The Oral History of Kendrick Lamar's 'To Pimp a Butterfly.'"

23 https://www.instagram.com/p/jqXYYAwK_y/?utm_source=ig_web_copy_link.

24 Sequoia Maner, "'Where Do You Go When You Go Quiet?': The Ethics of Interiority in the Fiction of Zora Neale Hurston, Alice Walker, and Beyoncé," *Meridians* 17, no. 1 (September 1, 2018): 184–204.

25 Frantz Fanon, *The Wretched of the Earth: Frantz Fanon ; Translated from the French by Richard Philcox ; Introductions by Jean-Paul Sartre and Homi K. Bhabha* (New York: Grove Press, 2004), 21.

26 Frantz Fanon, *Black Skin, White Masks* (New York: Grove Press, 2008), 146.

27 Joe Lynch, "Kendrick Lamar Talks Ferguson: 'What Happened Should've Never Happened,'" *Billboard*, January 8, 2015, https://www.billboard.com/articles/news/6436333/kendrick-lamar-on-ferguson-police-michael-brown.

28 Breakfast Club Power 105.1 FM, *Kendrick Lamar Talks Overcoming Depression, Responsibility to the Culture.*

29 La Marr Jurelle Bruce, *How to Go Mad without Losing Your Mind: Madness and Black Radical Creativity*, Black Outdoors (Durham: Duke University Press, 2020), 223.

30 bell hooks, *Killing Rage: Ending Racism* (New York: Macmillan, 1996), 26.

Chapter 2

1   Amiri Baraka, "The Changing Same (R&B and New Black Music)," in *Black Music*, 1st ed., ed. Da Capo Press (New York: Da Capo Press, 1998), 181.

2   MTV, *Kendrick Lamar Talks About "u," His Depression & Suicidal Thoughts* (MTV News, 2015), https://www.youtube.com/watch?v=Hu4Pz9PjolI&list=WL&index=100.

3   Nicole R. Fleetwood, *On Racial Icons: Blackness and the Public Imagination*, Pinpoints: Complex Topics, Concise Explanations 2 (New Brunswick, NJ: Rutgers University Press, 2015), 8.

4   Michael P. Jeffries, *Thug Life: Race, Gender, and the Meaning of Hip-Hop* (Chicago, IL: University of Chicago Press, 2011), 14.

5   Gwendolyn D. Pough, "Seeds and Legacies : Tapping the Potential in Hip-Hop," in *The Hip-Hop Studies Reader*, 1st ed., ed. Murray Forman and Mark Anthony Neal (New York: Routledge, 2004), 287.

6   The Editors of Vibe Magazine, *Tupac Amaru Shakur, 1971– 1996* (New York: Crown Publishers, Inc., 1997), 21.

7   Seneca Vaught, "Tupac's Law: Incarceration, T.H.U.G.L.I.F.E., and the Crisis of Black Masculinity," *Spectrum: A Journal on Black Men* 2, no. 2 (2014): 87–115.

8   Karin L. Stanford, "Keepin' It Real in Hip Hop Politics: A Political Perspective of Tupac Shakur," *Journal of Black Studies* 42, no. 1 (2011): 15.

9   Ibid., 10.

10 For the story of Afeni Shakur's imprisonment in the Women's House of Detention before eventual acquittal, see Bin Dhoruba Wahad, *Look for Me in the Whirlwind:*

From the Panther 21 to 21st-Century Revolutions (Oakland, CA: PM Press, 2017) and Jasmine Guy, "Love and Power," *Afeni Shakur: Evolution of a Revolutionary*, 1st ed., ed. Atria Books hardcover (New York: Atria Books, 2004), 69–89.

11 See Tayannah Lee McQuillar and Freddie Lee Johnson, "Black Royalty and Big Plans," *Tupac Shakur: The Life and Times of an American Icon*, 1ˢᵗ ed., ed. Da Capo Press (Cambridge, MA: Da Capo Press, 2010), 217–223.

12 1991 Interview with 2Pac by Davey D, published in Jake Brown's *Tupac Shakur (2-Pac) in the Studio: The Studio Years (1989–1996)* (Phoenix, Az: Colossus Books, 2005), 16.

13 See Michael Eric Dyson's *Holler If You Hear Me* (2006), McQuillar and Johnson's, *Tupac Shakur: The Life and Times of an American Icon* (2010) and the film *Thug Angel* for the most comprehensive accounts of Tupac's life and influence.

14 Joan Morgan, *When Chickenheads Come Home to Roost: My Life as a Hip-Hop Feminist* (New York: Simon & Schuster, 1999), 80.

15 Foe Tha Outlaw, *2PAC MTV Interview* (YouTube, 1994), https://www.youtube.com/watch?v=pNSRx14s7B4.

16 For a discussion of regionality in hip-hop culture, see Murray Forman, *The 'hood Comes First: Race, Space, and Place in Rap and Hip-Hop*, Music/Culture (Middletown, CT: Wesleyan University Press, 2002).

17 Kevin Powell, "This Thug's Life," in *Tupac Amaru Shakur, 1971–1996*, ed. The Editors of Vibe Magazine (New York: Crown Publishers, Inc., 1997), 25.

18 Hale, "The Oral History of Kendrick Lamar's 'To Pimp a Butterfly.'"

19   Frazier Tharpe, "Director X Breaks Down Kendrick Lamar's 'King Kunta' Video," *Complex*, April 3, 2015, https://www .complex.com/music/2015/04/director-x-king-kunta-interview.

20   Ibid.

21   2Pac, "I Wonder if Heaven Got a Ghetto," *R U Still Down?* (Santa Monica, CA: Interscope Records, 1997).

22   Larry Buchanan, Quoctrung Bui, and Jugal K. Patel, "Black Lives Matter May Be the Largest Movement in U.S. History," *The New York Times*, July 3, 2020, sec. U.S., https://www .nytimes.com/interactive/2020/07/03/us/george-floyd-protests -crowd-size.html.

23   https://mappingpoliceviolence.org/2015.

24   One9 and Erik Parker, "Alright: 2015," *Hip-Hop: The Songs That Shook America* (AMC, September 29, 2020).

25   Jayson Greene, "Best New Track: 'Alright' by Kendrick Lamar," *Pitchfork* (blog), July 1, 2015, https://pitchfork.com/reviews/ tracks/17553-kendrick-lamar-alright/.

26   I am thinking of Kevin Quashie's writing on the subject of black aliveness and worldmaking. He argues that "aliveness is the repertoire of having an ethical orientation in a world that is not ethically oriented" (154). See *Black Aliveness, or a Poetics of Being*. Black Outdoors: Innovations in the Poetics of Study. Durham: Duke University Press, 2021.

27   Andres Tardio, "Exclusive: We Got All The Answers About Kendrick Lamar's 'Alright' Video," *MTV News*, June 30, 2015, http://www.mtv.com/news/2201127/kendrick-lamar-alright -video-colin-tilley/.

28   Jon Swaine, Oliver Laughland, and Ciara McCarthy, "Young Black Men Killed by US Police at Highest Rate in Year of

1,134 Deaths," *The Guardian*, December 31, 2015, sec. US news, http://www.theguardian.com/us-news/2015/dec/31/the -counted-police-killings-2015-young-black-men.

29   Shana L. Redmond, *Anthem: Social Movements and the Sound of Solidarity in the African Diaspora* (New York: New York University Press, 2013), 2.

30   Touré, "An In-Depth Conversation with Kendrick Lamar," *I-D* (blog), October 16, 2017, https://i-d.vice.com/en_uk/article/ j5gwk7/an-in-depth-conversation-with-kendrick-lamar.

31   Jacques Derrida, *Specters of Marx: the State of the Debt, the Work of Mourning, and the New International* (New York, London: Routledge, 1994), 114.

32   Sharon P. Holland, "Bill T. Jones, Tupac Shakur and the (Queer) Art of Death," *Callaloo* 23, no. 1 (2000): 384.

Chapter 3

1   Konbini, *Interview Extract with Kendrick Lamar*, 2015, https:// fb.watch/7fasJww46i/.

2   Touré, "An In-Depth Conversation with Kendrick Lamar."

3   2Pac, "Changes," *2Pac's Greatest Hits*. Death Row Records/ Interscope Records, 1998.

4   Kendrick Lamar, "Mortal Man," *To Pimp a Butterfly* (TDE; Aftermath; Interscope, 2015).

5   Peters, Ken. *Tupac Uncensored and Uncut: The Lost Prison Tapes*. Flatiron Film Company, 2011.

6   Ta-Nehisi Coates, *We Were Eight Years in Power: An American Tragedy*, 1st ed. (New York: One World, 2017), 23.

7   One9 and Erik Parker, "Alright: 2015."

8   Thomas Hobbs, "The History of the West Coast Get Down, LA's Jazz Giants," *Dazed*, June 26, 2020, https://www.dazeddigital.com/music/article/49630/1/west-coast-get-down-los-angeles-jazz-collective-interview.

9   GQ, *Kendrick Lamar Meets Rick Rubin and They Have an Epic Conversation*.

10 Ibid.

11 Breakfast Club Power 105.1 FM, *Kendrick Lamar Talks Overcoming Depression, Responsibility to the Culture*.

12 Hobbs, "The History of the West Coast Get Down, LA's Jazz Giants."

13 Marcus J. Moore, *The Butterfly Effect: How Kendrick Lamar Ignited the Soul of Black America* (New York: Atria Books, 2020), 172.

14 Dave Chappelle, "Kendrick Lamar by Dave Chappelle," *Interview Magazine*, July 12, 2017, https://www.interviewmagazine.com/music/kendrick-lamar-cover.

15 Christina Elizabeth Sharpe, *In the Wake: On Blackness and Being* (Durham: Duke University Press, 2016).

16 Recording Academy, *Kendrick Lamar Nomination Interview | 58th GRAMMYs*.

17 Édouard Glissant and J. Michael Dash, *Caribbean Discourse: Selected Essays*, CARAF Books (Charlottesville, VA: University Press of Virginia, 1999).

18 Recording Academy, *Kendrick Lamar Nomination Interview | 58th GRAMMYs*.

19 GQ, *Kendrick Lamar Meets Rick Rubin and They Have an Epic Conversation*.

20 Shira Karsen, "Kendrick Lamar's Stylist Shares the Hidden Messages in His Grammys Performance: Exclusive," *Billboard*, February 22, 2016, https://www.billboard.com/articles/news/6882840/kendrick-lamar-stylist-grammys-performance-hidden-messages.

21 Hale, "The Oral History of Kendrick Lamar's 'To Pimp a Butterfly.'"

22 Richard Iton, *In Search of the Black Fantastic: Politics and Popular Culture in the Post-Civil Rights Era*, Transgressing Boundaries (Oxford ; New York: Oxford University Press, 2008).

23 Michel-Rolph Trouillot, *Silencing the Past: Power and the Production of History*, Nachdr. (Boston, MA: Beacon Press, 2011), 228.

24 https://twitter.com/ava/status/699427713115770880?ref_src=twsrc%5Etfw%7Ctwcamp%5Etweetembed%7Ctwterm%5E699427713115770880%7Ctwgr%5E%7Ctwcon%5Es1_c10&ref_url=https%3A%2F%2Fpublish.twitter.com%2F%3Fquery%3Dhttps3A2F2Ftwitter.com2Fava2Fstatus2F699427713115770880widget%3DTweet.

25 2Pac, "Keep Ya Head Up," *Strictly 4 My N.I.G.G.A.Z* (Interscope Records, 1993).

26 Hale, "The Oral History of Kendrick Lamar's 'To Pimp a Butterfly.'"

27 Ibid.

28 Toni Morrison, *Beloved* (New York: Vintage International, 2004).

29 hooks, *Killing Rage*, 120.

30 Baraka, "The Changing Same (R&B and New Black Music)," 195.

31 GQ, *Kendrick Lamar Meets Rick Rubin and They Have an Epic Conversation* (Malibu, CA: Shangri-La Studio, 2016), https://www.youtube.com/watch?v=4lPD5PtqMiE.

32 97.1 AMP, *Kendrick Lamar Talks 'i,' Next Album with Carson Daly of 97.1 AMP Radio*, September 23, 2014, https://www.youtube.com/watch?v=fwbV5eUCePs.

33 Ibid.

34 Derived from the terminology of Mark Anthony Neal who uses "post-soul" to describe the "political, social, and cultural experiences of the African-American community since the end of the civil rights and Black Power movements." See *Soul Babies: Black Popular Culture and the Post-Soul Aesthetic* (New York: Routledge, 2002).

35 "To Live and Die in L.A." *The Don Killuminati: The 7 Day Theory*. Death Row / Interscope, 1996.

36 The Isley Brothers, having been in the music industry for over sixty years, remain a vital vein between soul and hip-hop. According to front man Ronald Isley, the group has been sampled over 900 times, most notably by Public Enemy ("Fight the Power"), Naughty by Nature ("Hip Hop Hooray"), The Notorious B.I.G. ("Big Poppa"), Ice Cube ("It Was A Good Day"), Bone Thugs N Harmony ("Tha Crossroads"), and now, Kendrick Lamar ("i").

37 Ice-T, *The Ice Opinion: Ice T*, 20.

Afterword

1 Ralph Ellison, *Invisible Man* (New York: Vintage International, 1980), 13.

2   W. E. B. Du Bois, "Of Our Spiritual Strivings," *The Souls of Black Folk (1903)*, ed. Henry Louis Gates, Jr. and Arnold Rampersand (Oxford ; New York: Oxford University Press, 2007), 2–8.

3   Touré, "An In-Depth Conversation with Kendrick Lamar."

4   Ellison, *Invisible Man*, 508.

5   Kathy Lou Schultz, *The Afro-Modernist Epic and Literary History: Tolson, Hughes, Baraka*, 1st ed., Modern and Contemporary Poetry and Poetics (New York: Palgrave Macmillan, 2013).

Special Thanks

Many people have been integral to the development of this project from seminar paper to dissertation to book, including Helena Woodard, Tony Bolden, Mickey New, Douglas Kearney, Roberto Tejada, Evie Shockley, Kevin Quashie, Nicole Hodges-Persley, Regina Mills, Anne Stewart, Mickey New, Jean Phillipe Marcoux, Alex Lockett, Jennifer Wilks, Chad Bennett, Lisa L. Moore, McKinley Melton, Tara Betts, Amanda Johnston, Emily Ruth Rutter, darlene anita scott, Roger Reeves, and Ananias Johnson. I thank Yvette DeChavez for our *Freestyle Fridays*, and I thank my students for learning with me in our Critical Hip-Hop Studies classes. This book was possible with the generous support of several programs and institutions, including Andrew W. Mellon Fellowship, the University of Texas at Austin, Southwestern University, Spelman College, the Hip-Hop Archive & Research Institute at Harvard's Hutchins Center, and NEH Summer Institute: Black Arts after the Black Arts Movement. The musicians and writers who shaped my mind—who would I be without you? Keith Woodard, my forever lover—where would I be without you?

Also Available in the Series

ALSO AVAILABLE IN THE SERIES